Moving to LA for Acting

A Comprehensive Guide for Out of Town Actors Who are Considering Moving to Los Angeles

By:

Tom Gurnee

Dedicated to Buster Groovedog

Until we meet again my beloved friend and companion.

Moving to LA for Acting
A Comprehensive Guide for Out of Town Actors who are Considering Moving to
Los Angeles

ISBN-13: 978-1536896732
ISBN-10: 153689673X

Acknowledgements

As much as we sometimes believe we can make it alone, in this town, this just is not true.

In creating this book, I would like to thank Tom Ardavany and the Approach Studios for helping me make the move to LA, Lisa Ann Wilson for her wonderful illustrations, Chad Glass for his superb artwork, Bill Paxton for his kind words that keep me going and Stephen Mitchell for his friendship, mentoring and supreme knowledge on everything that's Hollywood.

Contents

Part 1 - Pre-Planning

Part 2 - Welcome to Los Angeles. Now What?

Part I

Pre-Planning

Welcome!

Well hello! Welcome and thank you for purchasing my book! So you have aspirations of moving to Los Angeles and becoming an actor. Wonderful! Believe me, LA is a great place and the city welcomes you with open arms. There's so much to do and see you could spend years living here and still not experience a large amount of what the area has to offer you. The acting world here is just as exciting and enticing. It's intense, it's fun, it pays, it's hard work, it's just about everything you could imagine it to be and it's all wrapped up, right here, waiting for you to sink your teeth into.

As for me, I moved here over four years ago from San Diego and I am still taken aback when I find myself in the middle of a sound stage or am on location. Cameras everywhere, grips moving to and fro, the wardrobe and make-up artists doing their best to make me look my best. It's a wonderful fantasyland of make-believe and I'm so grateful to be going through this experience in my life right now. I hope I never get use to feeling this way about this place or the work that I'm privileged to do.

It wasn't an easy road getting here, though, and I've learned a lot along the way. In the beginning, it was hard. Very hard. The place I was scheduled to move into wasn't ready when I showed up with all my things in a U-Haul (sawdust was everywhere and the oven was in the livingroom!). After I quickly stashed all my things in a storage unit and began a long camp out on a friend's couch scrambling each day to find somewhere new to live, my car was then a few days later abruptly rear-ended on the 405 freeway. You bet I was questioning my decision and the universe after that!

Fortunately though, I was lucky to already have a few sympathetic ears to lean on and some established part-time work here, but going through all the rigmarole of finding a new place to live, while suddenly becoming a friend's unexpected guest, dealing with getting my car fixed and the insurance headache and negotiations that followed, finally getting set up and getting acclimated to my new environment (not to mention the 10% sales tax in some places – OMG!), took some time and I have a few battle scars from all of those things and more.

Yes, life had a way of "testing" me back then; making sure I was absolutely serious about what I was I was choosing to do with my life. Finally, I got settled into a pretty decent place, the internet was hooked up, my computer was running and my dog was happy and content. I readily dove into doing those things I knew I could do to get started in the industry (which wasn't much). Along those next days and weeks, I remember thinking I wish I had some sort of reference as a newbie to Hollywood to help guide my way.

I really knew nothing about the city neighborhoods or what a proper headshot needed to be look like, for example. I didn't specifically know where most of the major studios resided or what part of town I was going to be travelling to for most of my auditions. I had some experience with the daily traffic from the few times I had visited up from San Diego, but I really had no real concept of how full-on, all the time, LA traffic could be. Why were there parking signs and parking meters on practically every freaking street? Why didn't I have someone to help me mentally prepare for the expense train I was just about to get a first-class seat on…

And that's the major reason I have written this book. I've always been the type to try to help others and I've always believed that the more I can give, the more I open myself up to receive. So this book is for you. I'm here to help you stave off some of those, "But I didn't know any better" type of wallet drains you will come across and I'm here to give you a real and comprehensive dose of reality of what it actually takes to make it in this business. I want you to succeed. I want you to succeed while going down the straightest path you can find. So think of this book as your, "I've been there, done that already for you" module and I hope it will help save you some serious money and time over the long haul.

"I know Tom Gurnee as a friend and an actor with whom I've worked professionally. I wrote *The Question-Asker Chronicles* pilot specifically for him and he has a very professional approach to the craft and the business of acting. His *Moving to LA for Acting* is a valuable asset because, frankly, moving to Los Angeles is in itself a major challenge that anyone could use help confronting; add trying to launch an acting career to the equation and it can be overwhelming. It should be very clear that Tom knows his subject and cares that the reader has a successful result in making the transition into a new lifestyle and environment.

Enjoy the book and the journey!"

Stephen Mitchell, Director/Writer/Producer

So. Are you ready? Will you take a bite of the apple that's calling you to move here? Fair warning, reality is much different than how it's all portrayed on television. Will you take a bite without having a plan or being organized and then have this apple called Los Angeles take a bite out of you and spit you back out from where you came? Or, will you be serious about your career, be focused and do things right? If you are diligent and focused - and you're extremely lucky - the rabbit hole may just open up a magnificent, wondrous and abundant world that is beyond your imagination.

Organization!

Before you grab your stuff and throw it all into a U-Haul, take a deep breath. Yes, right now, and settle in for a moment. "Breathing" is actually an exercise many acting coaches teach. It serves you by helping to calm your nerves, by making you become "present" in the here and now and assists you in opening up those energetic channels that allow for creative flow and idea transfer. In a nutshell, it helps to clear and calm the mind...

So, one more deep breath... Breath out slowly... Very good. Ok. Here we go.

Let's begin with your organization and planning preparation. And this is the key! If you're truly going to make it in this town, you have to have a plan – that is, a well thought out strategy on how to approach your goal of becoming an actor and you have to have ways on how to carry it out with great action and speed.

I'll be going into details within each chapter to give you better frame of reference, but for now, let's think about the overall picture of how you're going to get here, where you're going to go and what it's all going to cost.

Travel Distance:
So where are you coming from? Up from San Diego like me? Driving in cross-country from somewhere? Hopping on a plane from across the ocean like a couple of new friends I recently met? The best thing to do right now is create an Excel spreadsheet of cost-related moving expenses. Once you begin plugging in criteria and costs, when it's all said and done, you'll have a pretty good picture of what dollar amount it's going to take you in the short-term, as well as in the long-term to get and keep you here.

Most computers have a spreadsheet style software program on them. I'm PC based, so I have Microsoft Excel. Please, at this time, go into your spreadsheet program, create and open and new spreadsheet, and plug in your first subject:

Gasoline: If you're driving, at the time of my authoring this book, in LA the average cost of a gallon of gasoline is $3.25 for regular. When something negative happens in the oil marketplace, LA gas prices quickly skyrocket (in 2012, the average price of a gallon of regular was $4.25!). So, from the get-go, begin mentally preparing yourself for these high-price shifts at the gas pump. In places like Beverly Hills, Studio City and other high-end living areas, add anywhere from $0.30 - $1.00 more a gallon.

Now, while I hate to do this to you, it's time to do some math. We need to calculate how much it's going to cost you to drive from where you are to get here. For example, if your car has a 13 gallon fuel tank and gets 25mpg, then 13 x 25 = 325 miles on one tank of gas. Go to Google and type in "Distance Calculator" into the search bar and plug in the city or town from wherever it is that you are originating from and then Los Angeles as your destination point. Make sure you are calculating miles and not kilometers and voila, you have an idea of how many miles it's going to take to get to downtown LA. If, for example, you'll be driving some 1,200 miles, then 1,200 divided by 325 (miles driven per tank) = round about 3.7 tanks of gas. If you round out an average of using $3.25/gallon multiplied by your 13-gallon tank, that comes to $42.25/tank. That figure multiplied by 3.7 tanks of gas = $156.33. Hoorah! Your first expense figure!

Road Trip!	Gasoline	156.33

Time/Food: How long is your drive going to take? At an average of 65mph, 1,200 miles divided by 65mph is 18.46 hours travel time. Plan on eating during the drive? Subway was always a good place for me to stop and eat. Let's figure $8.00 a meal x 3 meals = $24.00. Add some car snacks for another $9.00. Total $33 for one day of food. But let's be conservative and say you can make it all the way on just that amount. Hoorah, your second figure!

Road Trip!	Gasoline	156.33
	Food	33.00

Other stuff: Gonna change your oil before you go? I'd suggest it. You're going to need your car when you're here, that's for sure. I use Mobil 1 in my car and that's pretty expensive oil. The filters aren't that much cheaper. But, you can get an average oil and filter change at the shops for around $25.00, plus or minus a few dollars. Ok, plug it in!

Road Trip!	Gasoline	156.33
	Food	33.00
	Oil Change	25.00

Getting the idea? Any incidentals you're heading out to Wal-Mart to go and buy for your road trip? Music? Sunscreen? Etc., etc... If so, plug 'em into your chart and record those costs, too.

Great job! This is organization. And you're starting to see already what your bank account is in store for when you make this road trip, yes?

Another reason I'm going through this, and having you do this, is for your success. I'm big into motivation, success principals, meditation, etc, if you haven't already noticed, because these things help ground you and clear your way towards reaching your goals faster and without impediment. Planning is so very important at this stage in the game. Without it, you may as well start throwing dollar bills out the windows of your car.

Reduce your plan to writing. The moment you complete this, you will have definitely given concrete form to the intangible desire. ~ Napoleon Hill

A good system shortens the road to the goal. ~ Orison Swett Marden

Plans are nothing; planning is everything. ~ Dwight D. Eisenhower

So! From now on, every time we progress into a new subject matter, be sure to plug those subjects and expenses into your chart and by the end, you'll have a solid idea of what it's going to take financially to make your move and keep you above the redline month to month.

Organize your Internet Passwords:
Another organizational skill that surprisingly few people employ is the consolidation of Internet passwords they use into one folder. When you get here to Los Angeles, you're going to be signing up onto a lot of different and new websites that are industry based and you're going to need new passwords to use to login. Storing all of these passwords in one place on your computer is a good way to stay organized and not waste time.

What I recommend is use another spreadsheet. In one column (column "A"), list the website name. Next, adjacent to that (in column "B"), write the logon name or email address you use to log into the site. Then (in column "C"), write the password into your third column. For safety, write just enough of your password so that you can remember the rest. For example, if my password was: "kennedy", I'd only write, "ken" and I know that the rest of the password is actually "kennedy". This way, should for some bizarre reason your computer gets hacked or stolen if you're using a laptop, they still won't have a way into these accounts. Next, when you go to name the folder you use to store these passwords, use something different, but not so different to attract attention to it. In other words, don't label this folder, "Passwords". Name it something fairly off the wall that only you would recognize it. Finally, use different passwords for different sites! You know why. ☺

Where to Live?

Los Angeles is one of the biggest cities in the world. It's vast, spread out from neighborhood to neighborhood and the traffic here sucks. Fortunately, however, the studios and casting offices are conglomerated into a relatively small area for our convenience. There are still distances to be traveled, but at least I hope you'll have a better idea of where to move after this chapter.

Car vs. Public Transportation:
Before I begin, let me mention public transportation. There is a public transportation system here in Los Angeles and it's actually fairly decent. There is a small subway system that runs in and out of downtown LA. Most larger incorporated areas (i.e., Santa Monica) run their own bus lines. Out in the Valley, there are dedicated bus lines and these lines run you into North Hollywood where you can make transfers to other bus lines and the subway. If, and that's a big if, you plan on using public transportation out here, plan on it being just like everywhere else. It's going to be slow and it's going to take a lot of time getting from point A to point B.

So, my question to you is, if your agent or manager calls you up and says, "Allison! You have to be at the LAX Marriott ("LAX" is the 3 letter airport code for Los Angeles International Airport and this hotel is located at the airport) in three hours to meet Spike Lee for an interview," and you're sitting on a bus, how's your mindset going to be if you have to get off, cross the street, wait for another bus to come to take you home so you can wash up, dress appropriately, then quickly dissect the public transportation maps on the internet to see how to get to LAX, hop on another bus to get there, make a transfer, and wait for that bus to come, etc.? Maybe you'll be frazzled, maybe you won't. But that story I just told is a true one. Fortunately, the young lady who received that phone call on the bus made it to her appointment just in time and got the part. She starred in an HBO series and, yes; I heard she bought a car.

But did you get the whole public transportation story there? That woman is freaking lucky she made it in time. Having a car is divine here in LA and having the freedom and flexibility to receive a call like

that (be forewarned, your agent <u>will</u> call you out with ridiculously short notice auditions like this!) and confidently knowing that you'll make your appointment is like gold. More
importantly, your agent <u>expects</u> you to make these appointments, and be on time, and rock the audition when you get there.

Obviously, it's your decision on having a car or not. But if you are interested, at the time of this writing, a one-way bus ticket costs $1.50. Day pass: $5.00. Same for the subway. If you have to park your car on the street at a meter, you'll average $1.50 - $6.00 to feed the meter (depending on how long you have to wait at your audition).

One piece of advice, <u>always</u> carry plenty of change in your car! There are parking meters <u>everywhere</u> in this city and you never want to get stuck having to park at one without having change to put into it. On that note, there are many new-age parking meters here in town. That is, they take credit or debit cards. But, be forewarned, when you use a credit card, oftentimes the meter will charge you a minimum fee (like anything from $2 - $5!) and if you're just stopping into a place for 15 minutes, the city will be happy to take this extra money from you. Most meters, however, don't do this, but it is up to you to tell it how much time you want to pay for. See the parking meter image below:

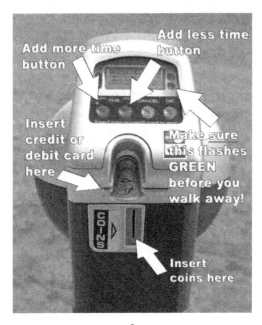

The image above is a typical Los Angeles parking meter that takes credit or debit cards these days. Slide your card into the slot, quickly pull it out and read the instructions on the meter. You can add or subtract time using the "more" or "less" blue buttons. This way, you don't have to pay the maximum every time you park. Once you decide how much time you want to be charged for, push the green button. WAIT for the "Approved" message on the face of the meter! That is, be ultra-sure the little light on the right side begins to blink green. If it does not, your transaction did not go through. If you leave the meter and it is not flashing green when you leave it, you risk getting a ticket. Parking meter tickets run upwards from $30 - $65 per citation!! No freaking joke.

Where to Move?
Do yourself a favor right now and go to Google. Type in, "Los Angeles movie studio locations" into the search bar. On the right side of the page, a link for "Map for Los Angeles movie studio locations" should appear. Click on this link and expand the map so you can get a full picture of the area on your computer screen. Notice where all those little dots are located and where the larger teardrop locations are situated.

Each one of the little dots represents a studio of some sort and many of these studios are ones where your casting auditions will be held. As you see, they are south towards Santa Monica and Marina Del Rey. There are dots as you go east into, on the south side, Culver City, and on the north side, Beverly Hills and West Hollywood (where UCLA is located). Continuing further east and north you move into Hollywood… North of Hollywood, they go into the Toluca Lake, Studio City and Burbank areas. And from there, there are a few that span westward into "the Valley" area. Finally, back south and east, you have a few scattered around the USC campus area and downtown areas as well.

Below is a copy of what you should be seeing:

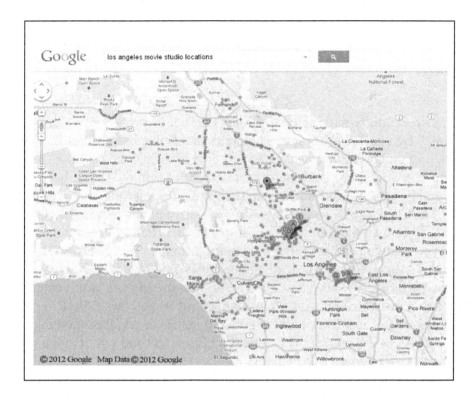

So that's your grid! Your job now, is to start doing your research on the neighborhoods in these prospective areas and begin pricing out living accommodations for yourself.

Things to keep in mind before your search:

Peak traffic times & Parking. Peak traffic times on the major freeways are from 6:00am (yes, that early) to around 10:00am. Sometimes until 10:30am. In the afternoon/evening, traffic starts to get heavy around 3:30pm and stays that way until 7:00pm – 7:30pm. Parking on any major street, and minor streets in high-congested neighborhoods, can be a major headache.

For example, in Hollywood, you should plan on giving yourself a minimum of 30 extra minutes to find a parking space if you choose not to use paid lots ($8 - $10) to park. When going out looking for places to live, search out and **LOOK AT THE PARKING SIGNS** along the streets. I cannot stress this enough. Street cleaning takes place on certain days and at certain times of the day. If your audition is on one of these days and in one of these areas, you better have scheduled enough time to find a parking spot because spots will be difficult to find.

Is the street you're parking on a "designated neighborhood only permit street"? **Be careful of these**!! The meter maids in these areas still work on Sundays! Have a spare $64 to give to the city of Santa Monica? Park on one of these streets without a permit… Also, **be extremely vigilant and notice whether the parking times say A.M. or P.M.** There are signs in Santa Monica where public parking is not allowed between the times of 7 A.M. to 2 A.M. That's correct and it's no typo. Did you catch it? Public parking is only allowed between the times of 2 **A.M.** to 7 **A.M.** Ridiculous, isn't it? Why not make it no public parking 24 hours a day, right? Ah, because the city won't catch you being unaware and won't make money off of you then. So, I caution you because your brain is going to be use to seeing something like 7 A.M. to 2 **P.M.** But if you park on this street and you're not a resident, you're going to be making a costly deposit into the city's coffers.

Weather. There is a range of hills that separate "The Valley" (the area north of the 101 freeway and the neighborhoods to the south - i.e., Santa Monica, Beverly Hills and West Hollywood). The San Fernando Valley is simply that, a mostly flat land depression that is surrounded by large hills and mountain ranges. This area tends to hold in heat in the summertime, as opposed to having the onshore winds from the ocean cool the areas to the south. The temperature difference in the Valley in the summer, can literally be 30 degrees(!) hotter, than the temperatures in the south. Last year, it hit 116 F in the Valley one day and when I drove south on the I-405 over the hills that separate the Valley from northern Santa Monica, it was only 85 F on the south side. On average, it will get into and stay in the 100's in the summer in the Valley, so if this is something you enjoy, then maybe this is the area for you.

Cost. Ah, the good landlords and landladies of the south know you want to stay cool in the summertime but alas, there's a price to be paid for this benefit – and you better believe they know it. Also, because these are the more climate beneficial areas to be in, this is where the swankier and more expensive areas of town are located. Beginning from the south beach area of Marina Del Rey, moving north to Santa Monica, then east into Beverly Hills and West Hollywood, you will pay on average an extra $150 - $1000 more per month to rent an apartment here, than if you were living north in the Valley or in the eastern neighborhoods. This is no joke. Small, one bedrooms these days in Marina Del Rey are renting for over $2,000 a month.

Living Space. This was a bit of a shock to me coming originally from Texas where we like things big. Prepare to downsize and live right on top of your neighbors who are on all sides of you. Southern California is one of the most tightly condensed living areas in the United States and the home developers took advantage of every square-freaking-inch they could build on. Same as everywhere else, we too have apartments, condos and houses to share and live in. We also have little guesthouses on properties. These are typically little studio style, detached, cottage houses adjacent to the main house on a property and many property owners rent these out to gain extra income. These are rare to find, but they do come available every once and a while.

Neighborhoods: One of the best resources I've found on neighborhood demographics is from the LA Times website. The following link will bring up a very well built, easy to use and interactive website that has a ton of information on all of the neighborhoods in Los Angeles County. Beginning on the "Neighborhoods" page, you select one of the 16 different LA County regions to the right of the page. For my example, I have selected, "Westside" from the list. This link now brings me to a page that lists all 23 individual neighborhoods that are contained in this region. On this page alone, you will now find demographic information pertaining to the entire region that covers population, ethnicity percentages, income levels, education levels, age ranges and housing percentages that are broken into rental vs. owned percentages.

From here, you click on an individual neighborhood. For example, click on "Brentwood" and the same statistics I listed are again sourced for you, but specifically for this individual neighborhood. In addition, there are 3 tabs you can now also choose that are found over the neighborhood name on the webpage to find specific information on crime, schools and comments made by individuals that live in these areas.

Below is an illustration of the website page and here's the specific link to access this demographic information:

http://projects.latimes.com/mapping-la/neighborhoods/

Neighborhood Costs: Neighborhood rent prices vary sharply from area to area so you <u>must</u> know your budget regarding what you are able to afford. Your best and immediate sources are:

Craigslist ~ http://www.craigslist.com   During my search for a place to live there was no better up to the minute pricing than from the direct renter sources themselves. Every single day, by the minute(!), new postings are being added.

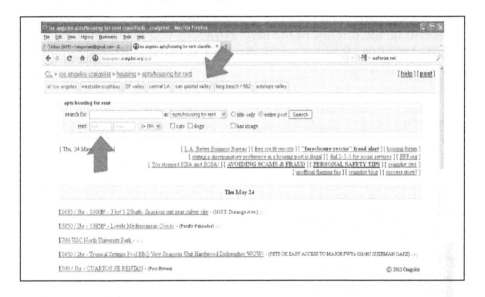

Do yourself a favor and be sure to winnow down your searches by using the area/neighborhood tabs atop the listings in the LA Craigslist Housing sections (as illustrated by the arrows). Using these tabs saves you time by segregating your search criteria to a couple areas instead of going through all of Los Angeles's postings.

As for these tabs, the ones you'll mainly want to concentrate on are, "Westside-Southbay", "SF Valley" and "Central LA". Any of the other tabs focus on neighborhoods that are, in my opinion, too far away for commuting purposes. Driving to auditions and acting classes uses gas and this expense cuts into your monthly budget (remember your maps and little dots of the studio locations from above). Save gasoline expenses, if you can, by moving somewhere relatively close (i.e., within a 5 mile to 15 mile maximum radius) to the studios.

Each individual posting in Craigslist typically has the neighborhood where the unit is located and you can reference these areas using the LA Times demographic link I provided above to tell you more about the neighborhood.

The Craigslist tab, "Westside-Southbay" = the west side of Los Angeles. If you're looking for Santa Monica and adjacent areas, look here. Don't venture too far south, though. Anything past Culver City or LAX and you're stretching your commute and using dollars. I've had auditions in Culver City but never south of LAX. The Westside areas will be the priciest of the neighborhoods you search in so be prepared for this. Rents typically for studios begin at $1,200/month and go up from there.

"SF Valley" = San Fernando Valley. Otherwise known as, the area north of the Hollywood Hills. Rents in most areas here are typically less than the west side's due to the temperature differences in the summer. But be aware of Studio City. Lots of Burbank executives and some celebrities live there and the rents reflect it. Mostly though, in the SF Valley, you can typically find studios that range from the $800/mo. mark to one-bedrooms that go for $1,100/mo. and up.

"Central LA" = Downtown LA and Hollywood areas. Downtown LA underwent revitalization a few years ago when the Staples Center was built and the area has blossomed nicely. However, traffic in this area is typically really bad most of the day because this is where three major freeways all converge. If you don't mind being in your car (a lot!) and dealing with snarled traffic many hours of the day, then some of the lofts around here may be attractive to you.

To the north, here you find the northern Hollywood listings that also include areas on the northeast portion of your search grid up to Silverlake. High-rise building studios start around the $800/mo. range and one-bedrooms from $1,100/mo. Parking is your most important and critical factor in most of these neighborhoods. Be sure to find out if the property has a place for your car and if so, if there's an extra cost associated with it (budget all this into your spreadsheet!).

16

If the rental space you're looking at does not have parking, your car is banished to the street and you'll have to deal with finding a parking spot <u>every</u> <u>time</u> you come home. In other words, how valuable is your time? If you're saving money by living somewhere that's cheap, that's great. But if you're having to use upwards to half an hour (or potentially more) to find a parking space, every time you come home, what is that time worth to you?

One final note about Craigslist. After days and days of searching through post after post, I decided to buck the norm and go on the offensive. Meaning, I put my own listing out there. I listed everything about who I was and what I was looking for (which in my case, most importantly, included a dog friendly rental space and my budget). Wouldn't you know it; I had a hit that very first day. So try saving some time when you start out. If you know the area you'd like to live in, go for it and advertise to that area and tell your prospective landlord or lady who you are and what it is that you're exactly looking for. Have them come to you. You might just find you'll save a lot of time and effort using this strategy.

Next, another very good resource is <u>West Side Rentals</u> ~ http://www.westsiderentals.com. Don't let the name fool you, WSR has an extensive list of availabilities in all areas of Los Angeles and you can directly access these listings at the bottom of their website. However, WSR is a pay-to-play listing agency. That is, you can't find out what the specific addresses of rentals are without paying a membership fee which, as of this writing, was $60 for 60 days for a single membership, or $80 for a 60 day dual membership. They also offer 4 and 6 month memberships: the single 4-month runs $70 and the dual 4-month membership runs $90. The single 6-month plan runs $75 and the dual 6-month plan costs $95. WSR is the favored listing agency of choice with renters and their listings are timely and accurate. (Don't forget to add this charge to your spreadsheet if you choose to use WSR's services)!

These listing services provide postings regarding people who are looking for roommates and/or who rent out single rooms (esp. on Craigslist). If you don't mind having a roommate or two, in the Valley and Hollywood areas you can sometimes find single rooms going from $550 on up. On the west side, usually they begin from $700 and go up from there.

During my research for this book, I came across a couple of other resources that I think are excellent to use:

PadMapper (http://www.padmapper.com) is a very useful site. It incorporates Google map technology and gives you an instant idea of where the property is located in the area of town you're searching in. The search filter to the bottom left of the website is very handy and lets you immediately focus on important criteria (like cost). What's super about this site is it is able to access advertisements from Internet sites and lets you know when these ads were placed (i.e., *"Source: Padlister, Added today (< 24 hours)"*).

When you click on the link that is provided after you've clicked one of the teardrop markers, you immediately go to the advertisement for the property that was placed. A menu comes up on the left side of the page you're viewing that allows you to save the listing or delete it from your map.

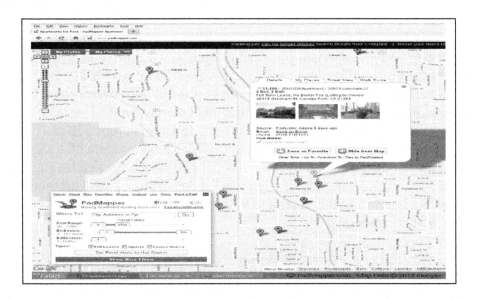

Within the window that comes up to the right when you click on a mapped property, you will see four tabs. The first has the details of the property, the second lists the properties you have "saved", the third, has the Google Maps street view available for the address and the fourth provides you with a "WalkScore" that ranks and indicates the overall percentage of retail shops amenities that are provided in the immediate area. Hence, you can get a really good feel for what's available in the vicinity without having to go there. PadMappers also has cell phone apps you can download and utilize.

The Rental Girl (http://www.therentalgirl.com) website is a smaller, more dedicated website. That is, it's a rental agency with live people in it to assist you. Different neighborhood areas (local "branches") are operated by a dedicated agent that is knowledgeable specific to that area and they provide free apartment and home rental listings. Their listings look just like you're looking at a property for sale. They include all the information you need and give you two or three paragraphs on the features of the property.

Hotpads.com (http://www.hotpads.com) is a locator site that incorporates some of the neighborhood demographic information I spoke of earlier. When you click on a specific neighborhood link, the page gives you rental-pricing statistics unique to that area. Utilizing the map technology to the left of the page, you can roll your curser over the dots, houses or tall cartoon buildings to have the basic listing information come up for you. Or, of course, you can utilize the search bars at the top of the pages to be more specific with your queries.

Zillow (http://www.zillow.com) is a site that includes maps and most importantly, the addresses of listings. The immediate information that comes up on their site is a photo of the property, the rental cost, availability (as in available now vs. in a month), square feet, lot size, number of beds & baths and whether they take pets or not. They also have free mobile apps you can download to make your searching easier.

Hot Igloos.com (http://www.hotigloos.com) The site is free and includes contact phone numbers and addresses. They have a decent search criteria tool and good Google mapping of their listings.

These are the best online rental sources I have found and I hope they serve you well in your search. Should you find something else that works quickly and efficiently, please let me know about it and I'll be sure to take a look!

Don't know anyone in Los Angeles and need a place to stay while you scout around? If your budget is flexible and you're in town for just a few days, try Airbnb (http://www.airbnb.com). Airbnb is more like a Hotwire or Travelocity site, but you can find a nice private room or guesthouse to use for your short stay. Each listing comes with many different pictures, large write-up of the property and calendar of availability. Prices vary widely depending on the neighborhood and these prices can be, in places, equivalent to those at hotels, but I have seen accommodations on the site as low as $25/night. Not bad for having your own private room for the evening.

A more lucrative option for your immediate budget may be CouchSurfing.com (http://www.couchsurfing.com). Couch Surfing has been around for years and has been an access site for people all over the world who are travelling and want to stay with others for virtually nothing. It's kind of like Airbnb, but you don't get a private room or house, you get someone's couch to sleep on. When I was living in San Diego, I had a couple visitors come and sleep on the futon I had in my living room, for example. Most visitors to someone's home are quick to depart after only a day or two, again, with the idea of just needing their host's couch to sleep on for the night and maybe a shower to start them off the next day. Hosts won't expect you to stay longer than two or three days so if you need to stay in town longer than that, organize another couch to sleep on. Be respectful of your host(s) and perhaps part them with a nice token/gift of your appreciation for the stay. You do have to register on the CouchSurfing website to participate.

Finally, here's another option to utilize if you are watching your budget. Try Hostel Bookers.com (http://www.hostelbookers.com). These guys show all the area hostels and you don't pay a service charge or a booking fee. I used these folks once and found a place near LAX called the Adventurer Hostel on West Century Blvd. This particular hostel had standard bunk beds and rates began at

$14.99/night (bring ear plugs; the metal bunks are creaky). It is also adjacent to the Adventurer Hotel and rates for these private rooms started from $45/night. The properties share a pool, free popcorn and 24-hour shuttle service to/from the airport. At the very least, the place is a clean and a respectable one to use as a headquarters to work out of. Obviously, there are other hostels to choose from in different parts of the city (there's one located a block from the beach in Venice!). Just be sure to do your homework, plan accordingly (you may have to book in advance!) on what days and how many days/nights you plan to stay and, of course, log these expenses into your spreadsheet.

Important Considerations: Here are some "little" tidbits you absolutely need to consider and take into account when finding a place to live. When using a rental agency, be prepared to fork out $25 - $35 for their "application fee". Application fees are basically little ways this town begins to nickel and dime you. When you're interested in a property, the agency and/or landlord will ask you to pay $25 - $35 to "process" your application and run a credit check. These are typically non-refundable fees and they do NOT apply towards your first month's rent. Beware: each and every time you put in for a property, and you're using an agency listing service, be prepared to hand over $25 - $35 for each different listing you apply towards. (Make your spreadsheet notation!)

Saved up your first month's deposit? Great. Now, get started saving up for your last month's rent, too. I wish I were kidding you. Here in LA, most places will require not only your first month's rent as a deposit, but your last month's rent as well. I know, it's crazy, but bad tenants have burned too many landlords in the past and this is the way they cover themselves. (Again, make your spreadsheet notation.)

It's weird, but there are going to be some properties you'll find that do not have refrigerators already in them. Keep your eyes open for this when viewing a property.

If your heart is set (and your budget is set) for living next to the beach, inquire about mold. The closer you live to the water, the more mold tends to be an issue. Find out what the landlord/lady has done about

21

this potential health hazard and when inspecting the property, look in all the nooks and crannies.

Not getting a good vibe from the landlord/lady? Has the listing been on Craigslist for a l-o-n-g time? Chances are there's a reason for this and it's probably not a good one. When looking around at potential living quarters, listen to your instincts. Really listen to your what your gut is trying to tell you because if your inner radar has begun to fire off and you're getting a weird, slightly uncomfortable feeling, it's probably the universe trying to tell you something.

When/if this happens and you still like the property, do some due diligence. Yelp (http://www.yelp.com) is a good place to possibly get a quick peer review on people and places. I read a story about a person that put in an application for a property but didn't hear back from them for three weeks. In the meantime, she figured out why by going to Yelp and seeing that 12 other people had already rated the landlord as being 1 star. She politely said, "Thank you, but no thank you," when they finally got back to her. Smart girl…

Check out Apartment.com's printable checklist and use it when going through the properties you decide to look at. It can help you mentally remember the important items that you decide you'll need when moving in. They're free to download and may be found here: http://living.apartments.com/printablechecklists/

Lastly, you, as a renter, have rights. Don't forget them and don't let landlords take advantage of you in any way (especially when you move out!). The following is a bit to read, but isn't your $1,000 last month's rent deposit worth keeping for a couple hours of your time? Get acquainted!

http://www.dca.ca.gov/publications/landlordbook/catenant.pdf

Timing Your Move

The timing of your move may or may not be important to you but here are a couple things to keep in mind.

Beginning in December, Hollywood typically shuts down the third week of the month (the Friday around December 15th/16th). Almost (not all, but most) everyone leaves his or her offices and are away for the holidays. Most productions are shut down by this time as well. Now, that's not to say a few commercials aren't being cast during this period, but most of the bulletin boards have only about 20% of casting call listings posted on them than they normally do.

Agents get back to work the first week of the New Year. However, I wouldn't recommend mailing anything (headshots, resumes, postcards) out this week because, as you can imagine, there's going to be a pile of mail waiting for them when they return and headshots from wannabe new clients are not going to be their priority. Mailing your stuff is probably best the 2nd week of January after they've already had a chance to settle in. I'm told by casting agents that this is the best time to be called in for an interview. They're looking to either add or replace some actors while getting ready for pilot season and they're not too inundated with their typical day-to-day activities yet.

Pilot season kicks into gear the 1st and 2nd week of February and goes into April. Agents will see you during this period only if you have a particular look or characteristic they need (they're still adding to their rosters), but they add at a much lesser rate than in January.

The next best time to do mailings is late March, early April. Pilot season has wound down and the industry is gearing up for summer filming, which, more or less, begins in May and goes through to October.

Filming typically winds up in mid/late October/November and this, too, is another good time to mail out and get an interview. But, be sure to do these mailings before the first week of December because that's when everyone begins to focus on you-know-what on the 25th.

I mentioned "mailings" for the most part because you'll want to coordinate your mailings obviously with the time that you set aside for your move. Plus, you'll certainly want to be up and running and organized by the time you mail out so you can be ready for positive responses. All in all, stay organized and schedule your move, if possible, in conjunction with when you plan to mail out to agents.

One last thing about timing. If you plan on using some sort of U-Haul or rental equipment, and you're moving towards the end of the month, plan in advance and get a secured reservation. Rental places tend to sell out near the end of the month because this is typically when people's rents are up. Stay ahead of the game and don't wait to the last minute trying to get/reserve a truck or trailer!

Cost of Living

If you're not already ingratiated into high living costs, like if you're coming in from New York or Chicago, then buckle your seat belt. Living in southern California means really stepping up your game and in all sense making a firm decision to make it here. Do you have a plan? Do you already have work waiting for you here? Do you have a nest egg to utilize? Someone to stay with while you get your feet on the ground? I really hope you do because if not, you're going to soon be suffering from major f-ing sticker shock.

Do you have credit cards? Do you have relatively high credit limits? Your credit cards can either be a blessing or a huge detriment depending on how financially responsible you are with them. Before you move out here the first thing I recommend is you call up your card companies and ask them to lower your APRs (annual percentage rates). If you have a credit card with a 12% or higher APR then you absolutely need to call your credit card company and ask them to lower it. Many times they actually will. If and when they do, make sure the new rate is a "fixed" rate, not a "variable" one. Get them paid down as much as possible before your move because the landlords you'll be running into will be checking your credit scores. All in all, you'll be using your cards to buy/book things online and over the phone and you may need those credit limit buffers to get you out of jam every now and then. I caution you, however. Do not let your expenses begin to outweigh what's coming in every month. For if you do, those monthly APRs will begin to slowly eat away at your bank account and nothing drives wannabe actors home faster than runaway credit card debt.

There's a tax those of us who live here in Southern California pay that is not found on anyone's law books or city code, but trust me, we pay it. It's called the "Sunshine Tax". You pay this tax in a lot of things and in a lot of ways but it's most predominant in your rents. If you're coming from the mid-west or south and you read the rent numbers I stated earlier, for as little square footage that you receive for those prices, you were probably shaking your head saying, "That can't be true..." Well, it is true and that's the Sunshine Tax in action. The weather out here is fabulous most of the time, and people who live

25

here don't want to deal with snow or rain or tornadoes or hurricanes. (We ignore the minor earthquakes.) The market is the market and prices remain at the levels that people are willing and able to pay.

Utilities are high. Most Craigslist posters looking for roommates advertise roommates to pay ½ of utilities at around $100/mo; 1/3rd utilities at $75. This does not include cable. Time Warner Cable, the predominant internet and cable carrier out here will run you $100 or higher a month for cable and internet. Add a phone line to that and you can add another $30 - $40. Sales tax is either 9.75% or 10%. Sucks, I know, but that, for example, is the infinite wisdom of city council men and women who think that, since you chose to live out here, then you can afford to pay for all the messes they voted for and got us all into. Most places in Los Angeles you'll have to pay for water; sometimes garbage disposal, too. Inquire about these as they can sometimes be negotiated.

As mentioned earlier, gasoline prices are some of the highest in the country due to the state taxes levied on gas here. Typically, a gallon of gas runs anywhere from $.30 - $1.00 more a gallon than in the heartland of the US. The best way to see how much current gas prices are in the area is by visiting Gas Buddy.com (http://www.gasbuddy.com) and typing in various LA neighborhood zip codes into their search bar.

Want to go out and see a movie? It'll run you anywhere from $10 for a matinee to $15 primetime to go and see it. That's just the ticket price. Popcorn? $4.50 - $5.00 for a small size. You'd think that with Los Angeles being the movie capital of the world going to see one would be a modest cost at most. Sadly, this is not the case.

Suffice it to say you MUST have a financial plan before coming out here. Budget, budget, budget at minimum enough money to survive for 6 months. More realistically, budget for 2 years! This way, in the beginning, your mind will be focused on acting not the immediate need to find money to survive and pay rent and eat. Seriously, if you come out here without much in your pocket or bank account, you'll be coming in here with not one, but both hands tied behind your back. If this is the case, realistically, how well will you mentally be able to get into the acting game if dark corners of your brain are constantly worried about money? Acting is going to take a lot of time and energy just to get started and if you're already placing a burden on yourself, what good are you really doing for your new career? Please, please, please do yourself the favor and really think your financial plan through. Stay disciplined and stick to your plan once you arrive and when you book a gig or two, reinvest some of your earnings back into your career. You'll be very, very glad you did.

Needs

Here's a little bit of information on some items that you'll need that are essential to your acting career.

Cell phone – Once you have an agent, you've just become attached at the hip to your cell phone. Agents out here will only give you so many chances at not being available to them before they drop you as a client (this is typically two times maximum). You do not want to miss any calls from your agent.

Computer/Printer – You must have a computer and printer to store information, store headshot photos, print off your resumes, etc, etc.

Internet – A must. A lot of your communication will be done via internet. A lot of your marketing will be done via internet. A lot of your self-submissions to the bulletin boards will be done via the internet. Etc, etc.

External Hard Drive – not a must, but certainly having something backing up all of your essentials for your career is not a bad idea. External hard drives are pretty cheap these days. You can find 500-gig or 1 terabyte drives for around $50 - $100 these days (plus that rotten 10% sales tax if you buy locally. Hint: order online).

GPS Unit – a must. Even if you're a local, having a GPS unit is a godsend. I can't remember all the different times my GPS has saved my butt by helping navigate me around nasty traffic jams or wrecks on the freeway. They straight arrow you to auditions and you can find parking in the vicinity without losing your way. Get one. You'll love it. Especially here in LA.

A Cutting Board – If you're printing out your own resumes (recommended to save money on printing costs), you'll need to trim those 8 ½" x 11" sheets of paper down to 8" x 10"s. A cutting board will help you do this quick and efficiently for around $10 at Staples. Buy your stapler there, too.

Remember, if you don't have some of these things; notate their prices into your spreadsheet. When you arrive, I highly recommend your immediately start up a monthly expense report. By doing this, you become absolutely clear about how much money is going out every month and to where. By keeping track of monthly expenses (like gas, cable, internet, food, rent, electricity, classes, insurance costs, phone bills, etc.) you stand a much better chance at surviving the long run and you'll be able to easily see how far and for how long you'll be able to stretch your bank account.

It's fiscal responsibility folks, plain and simple. Those that make it out here, stay out of debt and manage their expenses. Those who don't either go home, borrow helter skelter from anyone they can or wind up bankrupt. It's an easy thing to do here, people. Between class expenses to headshots to acting bulletin board memberships, to gas expenses running from audition to audition, to rent, to a night out or two or three a month, to your car payment, to insurance costs for your car, to Obamacare, to utility costs, to your phone bill, etc., the next thing you know your forking out $2,000/month just to get by and live day to day. You must, must, must stay diligent with your monthly expenses or this town will eat you alive. Don't ruin your life (or your credit!) by making bad fiscal choices. Stay vigilant and stay on top of your personal finances.

What to do BEFORE you get here

One of the most important things you can do for your acting career right now, let me repeat: RIGHT NOW(!) is social networking and building your fan base. I'll be speaking more about personal marketing later on but I want to talk to you about social networking now because it is becoming more and more relevant, dare I say crucial, for a beginning actor and his/her career.

Social networking has become the norm today and actors must be utilizing these platforms to the best of their capabilities. That means, Facebook, Twitter and YouTube. What's important on these sites is to **begin building a fan base**.

I recently attended a seminar presented by someone who coaches actors on streamlining their careers. He brought in a casting director friend of his and the topic of social networking came up. Both the coach and the casting director said it is vital that actors build their fan bases. The first and most important reason you should build your base is that it can have the immediate effect of creating credibility in the eyes of those who can hire you.

Simply put, if you can go into an interview and you have a fan base of 30,000 Twitter followers, you're going to have someone's full and undivided attention. Similarly, if you can go into the interview and say you've starred in a short film on YouTube that has over a million hits, you're again going to perk up someone's ears. Fan bases mean money to those who hire you and that's the name of the game they're in – to make money.

For example, have you seen actors on the television that star in a series that only lasts one season (if that) again and again? (Which, of course, leads you to ask the question, why do they keep hiring the same actor to do productions that continually fail?) Well, these actors keep showing up because the answer is, in large part, they have a very large and loyal fan base. And if a producer knows that an actor can, at least and at bare minimum, bring in a solid base of viewers to start a show with, they'll be willing (again and again) to roll the dice with that actor. Or, as another example, perhaps they'll be willing to take a chance on giving a starring role to someone that has had numerous co-starring roles because they're starting to see the numbers are there to give this person a chance at breaking out on his/her own. It's always about the numbers and social networking is just another platform executives can use from which to make their decisions.

Getting back to the seminar I spoke of, the casting director that was present said, that when it comes down to deciding between two actors who she recommends for a single role, given the circumstances that all other factors are the same, she absolutely will take fan base into consideration. The acting coach was even told by some of his clients that agents have asked them during their interviews about their fan base numbers. Let me tell you, that comment perked up a lot of ears in the audience.

Another reason fan base is important is because the more fans (friends) you have, the more people help spread the word about you and your work. The more people that know about and/or find you, the more work begins heading your way. As I've mentioned before, it's all about networking in this town and using social networking platforms to meet people is simply a requirement today.

How do you create fan base? One of the quickest and easiest ways is self-produce.

Self-producing means utilizing what you have at your disposal and/or doing something fun that comes natural for you. You've no doubt heard stories of (or have personally seen) people on YouTube who broadcast themselves doing one thing or another online and their little mini-productions have millions of hits for whatever reasons. They've found someone with a camera and did something or told a story about something that resonated with a ton of people. Need an example? Just go to YouTube's homepage and check out the latest uploads that have hundreds of thousands of hits already. In fact, as I'm looking at YouTube's homepage right now, there are a couple of young guys in either their late teens or early twenties that are reviewing the latest movies that have come out. In two days, they're already over 250,000 hits! Digging a little deeper, their channel has had, omg, over 95,000,000 views, has over 406,000 subscribers and...AND...they joined YouTube <u>only one year ago</u>! Holy cow. You bet you see advertising on their page; which of course means...you guessed it! They're cranking and banking.

So, my question to you is, if you were these guys and you walked into a networking executive's office with this type of ammunition and you had a good look, some talent and obvious drive, do you think you'd have a chance at being taken seriously? You bet you would.

Folks, it's the same with Twitter and Facebook. I heard the story that there's a mom out there who just loves to Twitter her comings and goings about living with her two year old. For whatever reason, people love this woman and she has over 400,000 followers. Just for loving to tweet and saying something that people apparently like. Facebook: same deal. Start posting and get to that magic number of 5000 (Facebook's limit of friends). Then, if you run over 5000 friends, start a new page on yourself and work that up, too. Fan base people. Start it. Build it. Groom it. And do it now, before you get here.

Now, just a word to the wise (or, if you will, my disclaimer) when utilizing platforms like Facebook, use caution and use common sense. <u>Please</u>. It's ok to go out and "friends" people, but once you do become friends with a producer or another actor, don't immediately go out and friend all of their friends. That's just tacky and it doesn't reflect very well on you. If you become friends with a casting director for example, you always want to put your best foot forward and simply remember they can say good things about you or they can say bad things about you. Hollywood, believe it or not, is a very small town and word does actually travel around quite fast regarding people here. Be nice to people and treat them with respect on the social networks and they'll do the same with you.

YouTube and Facebook are obviously excellent platforms to market your latest and greatest work. Once you've uploaded a video you're starring or co-starring in, spread the word! Just keep in mind that what you post online, you post to the world. And if it isn't your best work, will you be up for having people see it and/or reference it in years to come?

People make livings creating content for YouTube. If you're creative enough and you have the means, skills and intelligence (and all of you do!), then by all means go for it. If, however, you're a little gun-shy or don't have the means to produce yet, at the very least (and for certain), you want your demo reel there (casting agents are looking for you online!) and you want to be able to link to it easily so you can send it out to anyone that you feel should have it.

So. In a nutshell… It's about numbers – it's about fan base. Self-produce, self-produce, self-produce. Hone your craft while you're creating and when you're ready, you'll be able to knock 'em out of their socks when you ride into town.

Intent – And, the Power of Positive Thinking

Before I get into the bread and butter of the business, I want to chat a little bit about your intent on becoming an actor. Intent is a very powerful word and when used correctly, it can open many wonderful and positive doors for you. For many people (I believe myself to be included) this invisible power can assist in bringing the right people into your life that can help you in one way or another. I believe it can help keep you focused on what's most important. Without it, you are, and always will be, a ship without a rudder. You will be one who wilfully allows the currents of life to dictate who you are, instead of being the Captain who takes the lead to control his own ship. Trust me, you do not want to be rudderless in this town.

Put another way, you MUST have a clear plan and idea on how you choose to create your acting career. If you do not, you will flounder and you will waste precious time, energy and expense.

There's a saying here in Hollywood: Every day, 6000 wannabe actors arrive in LA and get off the train at Union Station, looking to make their wildest dreams about becoming a star come true. And everyday, 6000 other wannabe actors get on those trains and go back home.

Ask yourself the question – and really ponder for an answer – What's the difference between those that make it in Hollywood that become working actors, and those that don't? Is it heart? Is it money? Is it luck? Is it talent? This question will really serve you if you will let it, but the key is to really think about it.

Perhaps you'll find there are positive and negative answers for the question(s) I posed (heart vs. money vs. luck vs. talent). One could say a wannabe actor had all of those things, but something was missing and he still ended up back on the train.

There are so many actors here the numbers truly will astound you. It still boggles my mind when I choose to think about it. "Why am I here competing against thousands of people who look just like me?" "Why did he/she make it when he/she looks/acts/talks like such an idiot? He/she can't act. Anyone could act better than that!" But yet, they still got the role and you did not. What were you missing that they had? Maybe you were a better actor. Maybe you did have a better look. But the door opened for them and not for you…

This town is funny like that. You'll audition for a commercial and then see that commercial later on television and go, "WTF? They cast *him/her* for the role?! He's/She's so dull…" It'll happen...

The answer is, who knows why they got the role and you didn't. Only the director who chose this person out of the dozen, hundred, or thousands that auditioned knows. Maybe they were extremely well trained and knocked the socks off of the director. Then again, maybe they weren't. You can speculate all you want until you're blue in the face but all that's going to do is make you angry, confused and negative.

As human beings we're all made of atoms, yes? Of course. But what are atoms? Well, in a nutshell, they're particles of energy. Hence, one can make the argument that human beings are masses of energy that are held together by molecules that have come together to vibrate on a certain frequency. We, as humans vibrate at one set of vibrations, while a rock in a field, or a tree, or a squirrel, or whatever you see in front of you right now vibrates at another parameter of speed.

The point is, it has been scientifically proven that we, as humans, generate energy. And, it has also been proven, that the type of energy we generate can have a positive, or negative, effect upon us. When we have good and great days and are positive and full of good spirits, we, as some would say, "vibrate faster". When we're down in the dumps or angry, we vibrate at a lower speed. You've heard of the Law of Attraction? Seen, "The Secret"? Well, this is another part of that. Universal Law, as those who are knowledgeable in the metaphysical world would teach, says that like, attracts like. More scientifically speaking, the speed at which you are vibrating, attracts that same speed of vibration back to you.

Recently, it has also been discovered that thoughts, are indeed, "things". And because they are things, they serve to have a positive or negative effect upon us, just as all "things" do, whether they be

35

substantive or ethereal. Some very famous and very rich people have written many books on this subject. I highly recommend you look up some of these people (Norman Vincent Peale, Napoleon Hill, Bob Proctor, Tony Robbins) and read their books. Because what better way to emulate success than by doing what a successful person does? Start reading some of the biographies of your favorite actors and find out what they did to get their "big break"…

What all these books have in common is that successful people tend to have a lot of the same traits and habits. And two of these traits go hand-in-hand with each other. These two things are: the power of positive thinking and having a firm, focused and unwavering intent on what it is they you desire to achieve.

The Power of Positive Thinking: Oh, how I wish I could sit and chat with you and debate all the wonderful characteristics and ins and outs of this subject, but we, no doubt, would go on for days and end up writing our own books on totally different subjects other than acting. So, as you'll recall from the beginning, I wrote:

I write this with the sincere intent to help you with your decision making process and offer you an unbiased picture of what it's really going to take to move out here and begin making a living as an actor.

Hence, the reason I have brought this subject to your attention is to do just that. To bring the subject to your attention.

Have you ever really concentrated on the thoughts that you have? That is, have you ever really been conscious about what thoughts you are thinking? Do you really "hear" what comes out of your mouth sometimes? These are reasonable questions and here's why. When you concentrate on your thoughts, you'll be amazed at how negative, they can be. Either you're having negative thoughts about something or someone, or your saying or thinking negative thoughts about yourself… Most of the time we really don't catch ourselves in this kind of thought pattern. But then again, most of us don't really, seriously, succeed at what we set out to do, do we? And I mean, really succeed, to the point that you're considered a master or professional by your peers (as well as strangers) and you're now living a financially free life.

Of course, the word, "succeed", is a relative one. One can say they have already "succeeded" because they were born. Think about that. One, singular sperm from you father got through to and into the egg from your mother and out of all the other millions of sperm that tried, "you", succeeded. "You", are here now because you won the very first race you ever entered into – the one you never even knew you were in.

You are a winner. No matter what anyone, a-n-y-o-n-e says or does or thinks to the contrary. The only question is, do you believe it? When you do, the power of positive thinking is working for you.

Negative thoughts as well as positive thoughts will bear fruit. Conceive negative – achieve negative. Conceive positive – achieve positive. Positive thinking is the key. ~ Norman Vincent Peale

Ever known someone who's negative all the time? I think we all know someone like this. And there are two types of people who company with this person: One, the kind of person who thinks it's a real drag and feels bad themselves when they're around this person, and two, the kind of person who feeds off this energy and joins in on the conversation. If you know someone of the second type, are they doing well in their lives? Some will be, but I'd bet there are a lot more out there that aren't.

From David O. McKay's, Motivation for Dreamers:
DEVELOP THE POWER OF POSITIVE THINKING - THINK THE RIGHT THOUGHTS.

"There are many techniques that I have come across to do this. Some of the most practical are:

Expose your mind to the right things.
- Watch the right movies.
- Listen to the right music.

- Read the right books.
- Associate with the right people.

Stay away from negative people – they will drain you of your energy and drag you down with them. Avoid them like the plague.

Thinking right is not a quick-fix process. You cannot change 20-year-old habits in one week. You should not attempt to. It will frustrate you. Start slowly. Before long, it will become a habit to think right. Don't get discouraged if you struggle a little with it. It takes time. It is a lifelong process. It is a way of life. It only ends when you die. Persevere. **Anything that is not in harmony with your dreams and desires – throw it out**. Weed it out of your mind. Continually work at it and you will develop a beautiful mind. You will develop a mind that will deliver to you the power of positive thinking and all the lovely things that go with it".

"Your thoughts are the architects of your destiny".
~ *David O. McKay*

One of the most famous of all quotes about the power of the mind comes from Napoleon Hill and his book, "Think and Grow Rich":

Whatever
THE MIND OF MAN
can
CONCEIVE
and
BELIEVE
it can
ACHIEVE

When it comes right down to it, everything, literally everything, that has ever been crafted and made by human hands, was first a thought in someone's mind. The question is, how many people had this same thought at the same time and of them, who had enough passion and desire to see it through to fruition?

When you harness the power of your mind and your thoughts to work for you, and not against you, you will immediately raise your vibration and wonderful things can begin happening in your life.

How the Universe Works: Ever wondered why you never receive what it is you so desperately pray for? It's because you're "desperately" praying for it.

Ever wonder why when you "want" and "try" to do or get something, all that ends up happening is more and more personal frustration? This is because - you're "wanting" and "trying".

"The universe works in mysterious ways…" Yes, it does and here's an explanation to one of those mysteries. The reason you end up with frustration when you "want" something is because the universe is giving you exactly what you are asking for – more "want".
Did you get that?

I'll say it again. When you want something, the universe has no choice but to give whatever it is you are asking for. In this case, you asked for "want" and the universe gave you precisely that. More "want". In simpler and consolidated terms, whenever you say, I "want"…, that's what the universe gives you, more "want".

The key to how the universe works is this: It works backwards. Instead of saying I "want", you give passionate praise, gratitude and thanks in advance for "xyz" coming to you. By doing this, the universe, again, has no choice but to deliver this "xyz" to you. The more specific you are and the more energy and feeling you put forth in "seeing" (the power of visioning) "xyz" in your possession, the more energy the universe has to work with and the more apt you are to see a quicker result. You must be vigilant, constant and disciplined to keep this thought process and these positive feelings going for you. For if you do not, your desire will quickly fizzle and soon the ego (that entity that serves to protect you from circumstances – be them positive or negative – outside the immediate norm) will help shoot your desire down. Stay focused!

Of course, all that being said, I can hear you now saying, "Thank you for the winning lottery ticket I just bought at my convenience store." Well, what I have to say to that is:

God's delays are not God's denials. ~ Robert H. Schuller

Who's to say, that if you fully and truly, without any shadow of a doubt, know, with every fibre of your being that you won the lottery - that you just might? Not me. I've seen some mighty strange things in my life and am witnessing strange and beautiful and wonderful things happening every day. Anything is possible. Including your winning the lottery. Will you? If you put that strong intent out into space? I don't know. But, what I am saying, is that if you put an amazing and powerful and positive energy out there, you stand to increase your vibration and your chances at something positive happening in your life will increase over the masses that have mindless, unfocused thought every day. I'll ask you again. Are you being steered from what other people are telling you? Or are you actually thinking for yourself and making <u>conscious</u> choices in your life?

Why are wealthy and financially free people the way they are? Because they are in control of their minds and they have focused, passionate intent.

<u>Intent</u>: First as a noun:
in·tent
[1]   [in-tent]
noun
1. something that is <u>intended</u>; purpose; design; <u>intention</u>: *The original intent of the committee was to raise funds.*
2. the act or fact of <u>intending</u>, as to do something: *criminal intent.*
3. Law . the state of a person's mind that directs his or her actions toward a specific <u>object</u>.
4. meaning or significance.

Now, as an adjective:
in·tent
2   [in-tent]
adjective
1. firmly or steadfastly fixed or directed, as the eyes or mind: an intent gaze.
2. having the attention sharply focused or fixed on something: intent on one's job.
3. determined or resolved; having the mind or will fixed on some goal: intent on revenge.
4. earnest; intense: an intent person.

Do some of these statements and some of these words "move you" emotionally? …"The 'state' of a person's mind", "firmly", "steadfastly fixed". "Sharply focused", "determined", "resolved". These kind of words get you a little charged up when you read them, yes? That's positive energy working. It's working inside of you, and working outside for you. That is, when you have a firm and focused intent, you become clear and direct. Your mind becomes free of extraneous noise and clutter and all that matters is obtaining your "intended" result.

What comes next is an internal drive, a hunger that naturally begins to germinate within you. Consider the acorn. The universe has already programmed an intention within it to become a mighty oak. When conditions and parameters are just right, this seed begins to build up internal energy. When this internal energy cannot contain itself any longer, it breaks the bonds of its shell and hatches into a young sapling. Quickly now, it grows and drives for the surface to reach the light that in turn, feeds it more energy to grow larger and stronger still. Upwards, it grows and grows until one day, it reaches full maturity and blossoms into what the universe "intended" it to be.

The oak is lucky. It already knew it was going to grow into an oak. It wasn't bothered by any extraneous negative personal thoughts or unfriendly negative family member comments. There weren't any friends or foes saying unfriendly things about its dreams and it wasn't encumbered by laziness. No! Its pre-programmed universal intent was to become a mighty oak. Period. Full stop. And when the environmental circumstances became just right, boom! Off to the races it went. Sure, it had to overcome harsh rains, bugs, winter storms, dry spells, etc. But it persevered and became stronger each time, indeed, each day for the experiences. It didn't stop until it reached full maturity. This is how to approach your acting career.

Neville Goddard is another wonderful writer on the power of thought and intent. One of his books, "Awakened Imagination" speaks directly about having your wishes come true by "thinking from the end". That is, if you were already a famous actor, how would your thoughts be then? What will/would you think and do from "this" place? How would you talk? What would you feel?

I very recently discovered these books by Neville and have put his teachings into practice. I remember I was feeling in the dumps about a parking ticket I had recently received because I was in too much of a rush to see my friends and wasn't vigilant about checking out the street signs. Literally, a half hour after I parked, street cleaning began. What once had been a side of the street loaded with cars was now a clear one with only my car and one other parked up against the curb. And yes, there was the nasty little manila envelope tucked up under both of our windshield wipers. (Again, please let this be a lesson to check the street signs before you leave your car!)

Back to my point...I was feeling cruddy and in a funk as I lay down to bed. I hate feeling bad and I had just finished Neville's book so I said to myself, "Enough. No more feeling like crud. Let's just talk about the screenplay I have written that I want to get sold..." And that's what I began to do. I talked about my screenplay aloud and in bed. While I was doing this though, I was very careful to put everything in the past tense – as though everything had already happened!

Immediately, just as Neville had explained, my imagination began to take off. I began seeing myself as one of the actors on the ship I had written about and I spoke about how each scene "was" so brilliantly shot and how they all affected me. I spoke about how awesome it "was" to work with the other famous actors and the very famous director who had come aboard the project. Next, my imagination took me to opening night and I literally began to "feel" myself shaking hands with everyone around me in the audience. It "was" so amazing to see how many people in the audience were having an emotional response to what they were watching. Afterwards, people came up to me and "thanked" me for all the hard work I had done on their behalf. While I was thinking these things, my body responded and I felt so proud to have persevered for these people. My eyes began to well up and I truly felt like I was literally at the theater. That is, it was almost like I had time traveled into the future and "the end" of what it was I desired was what I was now living.

It was a phenomenal experience! Truly. And my imagination just soared! I felt so good afterwards. So what happened after my little "trip"? Two days later I got a phone call out of the blue from the producer I have working with my project. We hadn't spoken in over a month... Also, I received a text message from another friend saying that he wants to hook me up with a buddy of his who has contacts at the production company the famous director I want working on my project owns. And, he says to me, he couldn't understand why he hadn't thought of hooking us up before... Interesting, yes?

Let me put this another way. If I asked you to draw me a house on a piece of paper with a pencil, what would you draw? My guess is you already have come up with a vision in your mind of what this house is going to look like, even while you're reading this and can already see it on the paper. All you have to do is draw it. That(!), is thinking from the end. In your mind, the house drawn on the paper is already a done deal even before you pick up your pencil. This is the concept Neville is trying to get across. By placing yourself at the end of what it is you currently desire, and thinking and feeling from this place, the universe will open the doors to you and introduce to you what it is you need to have this come to be.

Neville's books sometimes are a bit Bible based, but the scripture within these works is used primarily only as reference points. If you'd like to read Neville's books, and I highly recommend you do, they may be found online and downloaded for free by going to www.archive.org. There, type in Neville Goddard into the search bar and his four books will come up. I recommend reading "Awakened Imagination" first, then, "The Power of Awareness" second.

Another great website to find even more on this man is www.freeneville.com. As the website states, there's over 1000 free Neville Goddard lectures, articles, videos, daily lessons, radio shows, etcetera there for you to dive in and indulge yourself with and it's all there to assist you with manifesting and making the universe go to work for you.

Please note, I am not advocating his book as a bridge to go find Christ, or Buddha, or Mohammed, or anything in any way shape or form to that effect. I am simply presenting to you ideas from people from the past that have used specific ways and means they have discovered that have helped them become successful in their lives and their careers. It is my wish, that you, too, find whatever it is you can to shorten the time gap between where you find yourself now and where it is you ultimately want to be. Just like acting, choose which knowledge and techniques that work best for you and go for it.

It's not going to be easy: Nothing that you've ever been proud of in your life was easy at first. Think about something in your life that when you first began learning about it or doing it, it was hard. But you kept at it. You worked hard at learning the basics. From there you persevered and learned more skills. From there you crafted and honed these skills into something really sharp. And from there, because you had passion and heart to reach a goal you set for yourself, you won. Every little ding you took along the way you got stronger and wiser. You learned. You developed. You created. You evolved.

Just the other day, my friend wrote to me about her Ebay experience. A year ago, she literally told me she was "scared" to do it. I did my best to tell her she could do it if she put her mind to it. Over the next couple of months, she asked me to help out by taking some pictures of some things she wanted to sell. I could see that she was progressing. She kept at it and learned by going through the processes. Her Ebay pages got better, her sales have risen and now, she truly considers herself a master. In fact, she told me she made over $40,000 last year.

Believe it or not, most of the actors you see in the movies and on television really did bust their butts for years honing and crafting their skills until one day, boom. All that positive energy and focus they put out was returned in the form of a minor role on a new pilot. And then that energy came to fruition and another larger role appeared and was won by them. And so on and so on until it was their name on the marquee and they were the one whom the magazines wanted to do interviews with. Never, ever forget, that anything is possible. The question is, do you have what it takes to make it so?

To recap: positive, controlled thought, combined with an insatiable desire, deep feeling and constant action, infused with focused and passionate intent to reach a goal is how to short-cut the game and leapfrog ahead of the masses.

Persevere:
Los Angeles can be a tough town if you let it be. It all depends on your perspective. You're going to have good days here, you're going to have some not so good days. The question is, will you stay mentally focused to persevere?

A positive thing you can do to help yourself is find a good coach. Find someone either in person or online that sends you stories that are upbeat and positive. Find someone that perhaps has some skills that you lack and can begin incorporating. Greg C. Greenway is one of those people for me. He teaches a course called the Social Supremacy Blueprint and offers tools on how to properly network and make yourself a standout in a crowd. Tools that an actor needs. He's not an actor himself, but knows many people that are and he related this great story just the other day to his online subscribers. Read it and take it to heart. What he said about the actor blew my mind…

"This morning, I had breakfast with an actor friend of mine...

He'd just landed a pretty life-changing role in an upcoming movie, and it struck me just how weird the path to success is...

My friend wasn't the most talented actor, he wasn't the best looking, he wasn't even the hardest working...

I don't mean that he was lazy, but he definitely didn't go to as many auditions per day as some other actors I knew...

The difference?

He stuck to it...
We both moved to Hollywood around the same time and in those
6 years, I've seen literally hundreds of potential actors come and
go...

All of them saying the same thing...they weren't able to get any
work; it's been too long; they're giving up.

You know what the crazy thing about my friend is?

This was his **FIRST** ever paid gig.

6 years...
313 weeks...
2191 days...

Without <u>ever</u> getting a dime for the work that he loves so dearly...

How many people would stick it out; chasing a dream that they
were getting NO money for that was literally making them broke?

Have You Got What It Takes?

Failure affects people in many ways, it makes cowards out of
even the strongest men...

But if you can train yourself to re-frame failures into "tests" or
another building block to your success, then you will get that
much closer to your dreams...

Thomas Edison, the legendary inventor, was famous for this...

He believed that it took at least 10,000 experiments to make
a winning invention...

So every time he conducted an experiment and it failed, he
knew he was that much closer to a winning invention...

He didn't see failures as something negative, but instead as a milestone to success...

How will you deal with failure?

You are not going to get anything you want without some failures along the way; the world simply isn't that crazy yet.

Some of my early business failed spectacularly. I'm talking serious disasters that left me so broke, I was re-using toilet paper and eating 20 cents tuna for every meal...

But within each failure, I learned something, and was able to use what I learned to help my next successful business venture...

Look at your failures as opportunities to learn.

Analyze them; study them; and then get feedback from others about them.

But most importantly...

<u>Never Give Up...</u>

Colonel Sanders of KFC had his recipe rejected 1009 times...

The Beatles couldn't get signed for years and were told that guitar groups would never work...

Stephen King was told by over 30 publishers that his first book Carrie was garbage and he shouldn't be a writer (King has sold over <u>350 million copies</u> of his books)...

I could go on forever, the list of outrageously successful people who went through insane amounts of failure, is endless...

The only thing left to say is...Are **YOU** willing to do what it takes to make **YOUR** dreams a reality?

Talk soon,

Greg C. Greenway

That was a hell of a story I read from Greg. Really powerful for me. Going six years without ever scoring a paid gig. Could you have stuck it out in this town for that long? Crazy. I don't know if I personally could have. But that is the game out here. That's how much competition you're up against. That's what kind of determination you may need to finally break through. As Greg says, "Are YOU willing to do what it takes to make YOUR dreams a reality?"

Greg Greenway has become a mentor of mine of sorts. Although we've never personally met, I have garnered a lot of information on success from reading the emails he generates and sends through his free subscription service. You can purchase courses he has for sale or just find out more about him via his website:

http://socialcircletraining.com

Part II

The Business Side of Acting

The business side of acting is just that. Business. <u>You</u> are the CEO of your acting company and it is <u>your</u> job to make your business a profitable and successful one. As with any business, you need a product to sell (you), and that product must be unique enough from all the others on the market to get noticed (your training). You need to know where to place your product to get seen so your consumer buys your product (auditions) and you need marketing in place so that others out there in the world know who and what you are about (headshots, resume, reel, website, etc.).

Your product (you) must be refined and up to date. You must be attractive enough (in all manner of aspects) to those out there who make decisions so that they'll choose you instead of someone else. Being attractive does not mean being skinny, beautiful and tanned. It's about being self-confident, projecting that confidence, being trained and being ready, at any time, for whatever comes down the pike.

<u>Self-confidence</u>: Self-confidence stems from a lot of different sources. It comes from how comfortable you are in your own skin. We're all different. We're all unique. Some are tall, some are short. Some are beautiful, some are not. Some are smart, and some are not as smart as others in different fields of education. Whatever you have, or lack, doesn't matter. It's how you proceed to project what it is you do have to others and how you make up for what it is you do not have that is important.

In this business, self-confidence is key. If you're nervous in an audition, guess what? It shows! And straight from the horse's mouth the way casting director, Mark Sikes, puts it, "Who wants to hire a nervous actor? Why would I take a risk on hiring someone that could potentially be a liability on set?" If you don't have the personal confidence to go into an audition and show everyone why you deserve to be there and to get the role, then there are a couple hundred other actors out in line that do.

So how do you gain self-confidence? Well, one of the ways is from feeling good about yourself. *Personal appearance*, for example, is important. Do you have excellent grooming habits? Do you dress well? I was actually stunned to hear in a talent manager's class that people show up to auditions and agent interviews dressed in old, faded, ripped-knee jeans and t-shirts. Their hair was unkempt and they looked like slobs. Seriously, they said! Did these people really want the job? Seems to me they didn't. So what kind of FIRST IMPRESSION are they presenting themselves with? Would you hire someone that came into your office looking like he just came off the street, literally? I probably wouldn't. And neither would these people. And guess what? They don't.

On the other hand, Talent Manager Mitch Clem, raved about how well and "put-together" a prospective client was when she came in to interview with him. He was very impressed on how well she was dressed, how she held and handled herself and what positive energy and confidence she projected. Other agents say the same. When you come into their office looking like you're "already" their high-profile and wealthy client, they're going to be much more apt to possibly take you on. In other words, come into their office looking and feeling like you deserve to be there and knock their socks off with your great first impression. Because you never know... The person interviewing you could wind up being the one person in your life that got you that one key audition that shot you on your way to the top because they believed in you and they went to bat for you. They took a chance and decided to invest their time and energy with you. Why ruin this chance right from the get-go by giving off a bad first impression?

Self-confidence stems from *being ready and being prepared*. If nerves start to creep in, then you have to know how to deal with this energy and focus it in a positive way to enhance what it is you are doing. If you don't know how to do this, then your nerves will get the better of you and you're doomed before you ever begin.

As with anything in your life that presented you with a challenge, when you were properly prepared to meet this challenge head-on, you probably did so with more positive mental attitude and self-assuredness. Being prepared comes from proper training and discipline. When you practice your craft in class and apply what you learn (wherever the opportunity presents itself!), when that audition comes, you'll know you can knock it out of the park.

> *Before anything else, preparation is the key to success.*
>
> ~Alexander Graham Bell

> *You can do what you have to do, and sometimes you can do it even better than you think you can.*
>
> *~Jimmy Carter*

> *When you go through hardships and decide not to surrender, that is strength.*
>
> *~Arnold Schwarzenegger*

> *You've done it before and you can do it now. See the positive possibilities. Redirect the substantial energy of your frustration and turn it into positive, effective, unstoppable determination.*
>
> *~Ralph Marston*

> *Leap, and the net will appear.*
>
> *~John Burroughs*

> *Even if you fall on your face, you're still moving forward.*
>
> *~Victor Kiam*

> *A strong, positive self-image is the best possible preparation for success.*
>
> ~Joyce Brothers

> *The harder the conflict, the more glorious the triumph.*
>
> *~Thomas Paine*

> *It's always to early to quit.*
>
> *~Norman Vincent Peale*

Headshots & Photographers

Headshots. Yes, you need them and yes, they have to be good. So next, of course, comes the dreaded, "Where do I get good headshots," question. Don't worry; I'm here to help with this.

Let me start by saving you money from the get-go. Do not, I repeat, do <u>NOT</u>, use a friend who dabbles in photography every once and a while. Even though you may end up with a decent shot, chances are it won't be current "industry standard". I'll explain this in just a moment. If it's not, you'll be wasting money on subsequent printing costs. Unless your friend is a professional headshot photographer, <u>with name recognition</u> among casting agents and directors, your headshots will be viewed as being sub-par and you'll be asked to get new ones.

Casting agents and talent managers are sticklers for this (I know, this sucks), but I can totally relate to where they're coming from. Casting agents, believe it or not, are very busy people. In between getting the dailies (all the new castings for the day), choosing and submitting their current clients for these new roles, making phone calls to lobby that the production schedules a time for their clients to come in for auditions, they make time in their busy schedules to meet with you. So, obviously, the best (here comes those words again) first impression you can make (and I'm talking about from your initial mailing now, not your personal interview), the better.

Think about it from an agent's perspective. If you were in their shoes, going through hundreds of submissions a week, wouldn't you get to know what immediately stands out and what does not? Wouldn't you get to know pretty quickly what quality of images are getting auditions and what are not? And of those you like, there's probably a certain quality about them that only a few photographers are able to capture. Wouldn't you get to know who these photographers were pretty quickly by recognizing their work and their credit on the headshot? Of course, you would. So can you really blame agents for not being choosy after a while? That's not to say that an unknown photographer can't make headway into an agent's world, but the photographer has to be able to bring out that "certain something" in the actor and this "something" has to radiate from the photograph they've taken.

That "Certain Something": The only way a talent agent makes money is by you booking an audition. (Remember! NO talent agent may ever charge you any type of upfront fees for their work. This is illegal! If they do, they are not a legit agent!) So the agent has to present a casting director with the best possible image of you that can be mustered. A talent agent can call and pitch you to the casting director (which certainly helps get an audition), but if your picture just isn't doing it for the casting director, they'll say, "Thanks. But no thanks." And just like the agents, the casting directors, too, see thousands of photos and they, too, know what works for them and what does not. Therefore, your photo has to be great.

A "great, certain something" headshot photo is not a posed photo. You will never get that "certain something" from a photo if a photographer sits you down in a chair, pulls a backdrop down behind you, turns you a little bit and then says, "Smile!" They may wind up being very good quality photos, but they'll be good "posed" photos versus having something that is natural, real and energetic.

Here's the difference. As I said, Here's the difference. A "posed" photo is simply that, posed. "Smile! Ok, turn a little bit, smile!" You can spot them a mile away. They're your yearbook picture or family portrait, fake smiles and all. But a "real" headshot photo has <u>energy</u> coming from the eyes.

The "certain something" I refer to is exactly that - your personal energy and thought that begins within your body and shines out through your eyes when your picture is taken. It's natural. It's "locked in". It's beautiful.

See the difference in the two photos? You can see the posed picture immediately, can't you? Well, guess what. So can the casting agent and casting director. But, see how the second photo grabs your attention more and pulls you in? There's an energy radiating from it, isn't there? There's something to the eyes that make you want to lock in and look at them a little longer. And that's the key! It's that energy that will make a casting agent or casting director stop for an extra split second and put you in the small pile of people off to the right to see, rather than the large pile off to the left that's accumulating at the bottom of his or her garbage can. What separates a great photographer from a good one is their way and technique of being able to pull this very personal and beautiful quality out of you.

Most great photographers I have worked with either are, or become, energetic people when they shoot. Their heart rates pick up, they tend to talk fast and they get excited. And they get even more excited when they take a great picture of you. What occurs is, they begin to have just as much of a positive experience taking the pictures, as you are being their subject. It's almost as if a connection between the two of you is made. When this invisible bond forms, and the photographer loves what he or she is getting, and you, in turn, are having fun, then you will tend to give them even more energy and what results are better photographs of you.

You should feel very comfortable with your photographer. If you're not at ease, it will show. Conversely, if you are at ease, it will show. Remember, it's that natural energy you want to bring up to shine through you and if you don't feel good about what's going on, you'll inhibit or block this energy from free flowing and you won't like the results. A great photographer will know how to direct you and /or give you commands on how to subtly turn, smirk, smile, tilt, etc. It doesn't take very much at all to do something with the hundreds of muscles in your face to make it change and it's these teeny, tiny, subtle changes that can make or break a photo.

Great photographers will talk with you during the shoot. The reason is, they want you feeling inner emotion and they're looking to bring it out so they can capture it on film. At a recent workshop, the instructor had us do a very unique exercise about how we appeared to strangers. There were about 75 people in the room and the instructor handed us a piece of paper with about 25 different "types" of characters on it. For example, these types consisted of all-American, the jerk/bitch, lawyer, neighborly, cheerleader, military/law enforcement, psycho, etc... Everyone stood up and began passing their paper to everyone else. Without speaking, the other person would put a check mark next to each "type" of character they thought you represented.

This is important because first, you want to know how others see you. When you've figured the top two or three ways you're seen, then you want to make sure that you're portraying that image, rather than that "type", in your headshot. What's also important is that during the shoot, you want to be thinking and talking to your photographer like that character. Why? So the natural emotions of this type of character come up for the photographer to capture. If your character is antagonistic, somewhat bitchy, then banter with the photographer. Is she sexy and playful? Then literally flirt with the photographer. Even if the photographer is a girl! By doing this, your body will naturally project these types of characteristic emotions and your facial muscles will respond accordingly. Your great photographer will thank you for this and you'll both have a lot of fun during your shoot. And have fun during your shoot! It's your money and your time! Why not have fun investing it? The point here is, if you're having fun, it's going to show in your pictures and that's a very good thing. Most importantly, your shots will more than likely turn out great and have natural and real energy emitting from your eyes. Your shot will be attractive and engaging to all who see it and it will put you a cut above everyone else out there.

Finally, I highly recommend that before you shoot with a photographer, that you either have a good conversation with them on the phone, and/or, even better, you visit their studio and meet them in person. Also, any reputable photographer out there will have a website. Be sure to go through all of their photos and see if you can "feel" for yourself, the energy coming from their subjects' photographs. If you like, or have an instant, natural reaction to a lot of what you see, you've probably found a good photographer.

Industry Standard: So-called "Industry Standard" right now consists of having a separate headshot for your theatrical work and a separate look for your commercial headshot. There are little nuances in your pictures that the different (commercial vs. theatrical) agents look for and therefore, most of the time, you'll need two different shots. Every once and a while someone gets lucky and can use one picture for both, but most of the time, count on the agents using different photos.

Today, everything is in color. Period. No black and whites. Your headshot will have a shallow depth of field and not be too smiley (all full of teeth). If you don't know what a shallow depth of field is, I'll explain in a moment. What's more important, if your photographer doesn't know what a shallow depth of field is, run away. If they can't explain this to you, then they're not a real, professional photographer.

Because industry standard today requires a photo to have a shallow depth of field, studio, portrait style photography won't stand out as well as as a photo that's using it. No white or solid backgrounds; no portrait style backdrops. Only these unfocused color blobs in the background are what the agents and casting directors like today.

So, what's shallow depth of field? Shallow depth of field is the background behind the picture's subject that is blurry and has color to it. You, of course, are the picture's subject and anything behind you should not be seen. The more blurry the background, the more shallow the depth of field and the more the casting agents like it.

During your interview with your photographer, ask what "f-stop" they generally use for headshot photography. As for "f-stop", in simple terms, the lower the number, the more blurry it will be behind you.

For example, f-stops of 2.0, 2.8, 3.2, or maximum 4.0 are good shallow depths of field. Anything above 4.5 or 5.6 (this is too high) is going to show something tangible (that is, something that has shape and form), in the background and this is a no-no.

Refer back to the photo examples above. Depths of field (that is, the blurred colors behind you – i.e., the photo on the right side) should also serve to enhance your face and skin tones and should not distract, in any way, from your face. You should be seeing unfocused color that helps highlight your face, not be a distraction away from it.

If the background is not fully blurry in the background, whatever it is behind you will be considered a distraction and your photo will be sub-par and probably tossed away. Some newbie actors like to have photos taken outside along brick walls. There may be a tree that's recognizable behind them. These are absolute no-no's. You do not want anything, anything, to distract the viewer away from your eyes and face. Beware of "hot spots" behind you. Hot spots are very bright, if not white, areas behind you. This is important because sub-consciously, the brain and your eye will always gravitate to something white and bright first, then something darker second. If there's something bright and/or white behind you, or there is a bright color that really has no point being there, you are distracting your viewer by taking their attention away from your face and on to something that you don't want them looking at.

Shooting shallow depth of field is tricky for photographers. The more shallow the depth of field, the faster whatever is behind the subject's eyes and nose becomes unfocused. Imagine if you will, that you're sitting in a chair, facing your photographer. Now imagine drawing a porous wall from the ground to the ceiling just in front of your face. Now, put your face up to this wall and tap the tip of your nose against it. Now, since the wall is porous and you can put anything you want through it, move slightly forward with your body so that your nose goes through the wall, but the rest of your face does not. This linear line, from the floor to the ceiling that starts at the very tip/outward edge of your eyeballs, becomes the focus point for the camera. When a photographer shoots at a very low depth of field, i.e.. 2.0, your eyes will be in focus, but the area starting from your ears and moving backwards, will not be. It's those 2 - 2 ½ inches from your eyes to your ears that can make or break a photo due to focus. Obviously, you want your eyes and face to be in sharp focus, but not so much from there on back and certainly nothing in the background behind you.

The point to be made here is, the photographer should have you sit with your face leaned in slightly towards them, a bit more forward than the rest of your body. So, instead of sitting up straight, as in having a perfectly vertical 90 degree linear line running up through your back from the floor to the ceiling, now, you're leaning in a little bit and this line (your head and body) will be slightly angled towards the photographer. This is so the camera's computer will focus immediately on your face and you won't give it the opportunity to focus on anything else (like your collar or tie). Everything behind your face will then begin to blur, thus creating those nice, colored blobs behind your body.

Photoshoot Costs: A good headshot photographer here in LA runs anywhere between $300 and $500 (make your spreadsheet notation!). Anything less and you're potentially playing with fire. Anything more and you're wasting your money. Jeff Xander, who is very well known in the industry and is considered one of the best photographers out there right now, charges $350 per session. Jeff has a background in fashion photography and is excellent at picking out what outfits will work with your face. If your wardrobe is not suitable, he has his own fashion line and has been known to lend a top or two to his clients for a shot. He will probably pop off around 400 images for you, give you 4 – 6 changes and you walk away with disk in hand (no waiting for your images). He only shoots one or two clients per day so this means he spends a lot of time with you and you'll get both your theatrical and commercial style headshots done. He does have a makeup and hair stylist that he works with for women that he can have meet you at his studio (which is in his backyard) and that is an extra charge. Men, he prefers that you do not wear makeup for your shoot. You can look him up here:

www.jeffxander.com.

Once you have your shots from your photographer, it's best to have someone from the industry (ie, a casting director or manager) help you to select which ones to use. Don't know any casting directors or managers yet? Go take a workshop. More on this later. Once you have selected which images to use, have someone with professional graphic artist software (I.e., Photoshop) edit your images before you send them to your printer.

Headshot Printing

Printing. Here's another area where, when you're in the know, you can save some money. But just like headshots, there are industry standards that the agents like and (yet again) if you're not up to spec, they're going to tell you so.

Regarding headshot quality, you'll see it for yourself when you go out on auditions. Take a peek at all the different headshots people have and you'll immediately notice the discrepancy in print quality. So, you have to ask yourself: Are you going to go into your job interview with a sub-par resume (aka, headshot), or are you going to immediately stand out by submitting something they already know is the best and (sub-consciously) tell them that you're a serious player?

Reproductions: One of the best places to have headshots printed is Reproductions: (www.reproductions.com). Reproductions is an industry leader in headshot printing and just like I mentioned before, you can spot these headshots from a mile away. These folks have excellent customer service and very good turn around time, which includes free shipping for California residents for any order if you choose not to pick things up at their office in Burbank.

Reproductions pricing is fair. What I don't like are their one-time "set-up" fees ($18 - $22), but the prices for the amounts of headshots you order are good. The reason I don't care for this fee is what if you have to change your headshot? Boom, you're out another $18. But, if your headshot is a good one and you need more copies, then they have you on file and you don't pay this fee. Their complete price listings are located here: http://www.reproductions.com/LA/guide.html

Aside from headshots, they do postcard and business card printing and they have graphic designers available to touch up your photo (at an extra charge). They give you a choice on what type of paper to use and their online services are very good and easy to utilize. You can design your headshot layout right there online and when finished, immediately upload to submit your order.

One last note and warning. When you upload your photo to a fine printer like Reproductions, **be absolutely sure the photo you have selected has been viewed on a computer monitor that has been <u>properly</u> <u>color</u> <u>calibrated</u>**!

What this means is, a computer monitor shows you what colors the computer is reading from your photo. But, if the monitor is not color calibrated (calibrated to true, professional color industry standards) what you see on the monitor may be off-color. That is, a red that you see on your monitor printed out will only be a slight shade of pink. A light tan you see on an uncalibrated monitor may show up as a nasty shade of brown when printed. What may look like a normal color, caucasian face may end up looking somewhat green after printing. DO NOT make the mistake of uploading your picture to a printer and then finding out afterwards that the color of your skin is way off. Though it may mean an extra $20 or so, if you do not have access to a properly colored calibrated monitor, having a color-corrected proof made before you submit to the printing process may save you $100 or so by your not ending up having off-colored headshots.

Overall, you can probably figure spending a little less than $200 for 150 headshots. (Write this down in your spreadsheet!)

I'll talk a more about postcard and business card printing in the "Marketing" section.

<u>Actor's Photo Lab</u>: Actors Photo Lab is another place that is recommended. (www.theactorsphotolab.com) What's nice about the Actor's Photo Lab is they let you print small quantities of photos. They can also do a free printed test print for you but you must come into their office to pick it up. They can email you a proof, but again, be sure your computer's monitor is properly color-calibrated. Use this service if you just want to check format and layout. They do have a one-time fee of $10 for new photos, or $25 if you care to customize your name on your headshots instead of using their listed and available font styles.

Besides headshots, they do postcards, zed (modeling) cards and business cards. They also offer pre-cut 8x10 resume paper, resume printing and graphic design services. On orders of 100 or more headshots, they offer free shipping. On orders of under $100, they charge a flat fee of $8. Check out their website for the latest on their services and charges.

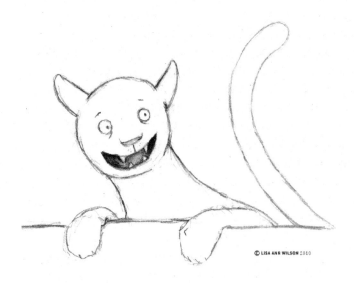

© LISA ANN WILSON 2010

Resume Format

Your resume format is another area industry standard dictates you conform. Although you have a little (and I stress "little") leeway in glamorizing up your resume, anything under your first heading should use the industry-standardized format from that point on.

At the top, centered, is your name. If you are in a union or SAG (Screen Actors Guild) or SAG-eligible, you should type this directly under your name in parenthesis. To the right or left, should go your personal contact information and opposite of that should list: your height, weight, hair color and eye color. Finally, leave a little room somewhere for your agency information to go, if and when you secure an agent.

Your personal contact information should be your direct phone number(s) and an email address. As for your personal characteristics, listing these things is a bit of a holdover from the old, black and white headshot days but still must be present. People ask why list your hair and eye color if the photo is in color? The answer is, that's just the way your agent and casting directors want it. So go with it. Women, don't fudge more than 10 pounds on your weight. You never know what they're going to be casting for and if you've listed your weight as being something under what they're looking for, then you might accidentally cost yourself an audition.

From here, you list your credits. In order of importance:

- Film
- T.V.
- New Media
- Industrial
- Theatre
- Training

1) **Film**: List any and all film credits here. This includes full feature and short films you've done. List three columns. Begin in the left column with the name of the production, followed by (to the right side) your center column that lists the name of the role

you played, followed by your third column to the far right which you can either state the production company name, or the director's name. It should look something similar to this:

Tom Gurnee
(SAG Eligible)

Height: 5' 10"
Weight: 150
Hair: Brown
Eyes: Hazel

Phone: 310 - 123 - 4567
Email:
  contact@movingtolaforacting.com
Representation:
  Your Agency Name Here
  310 - 123 - 4567

Film:

KingBreaker (Supporting)	Frank (The Bomber)	Matt Snead Productions
Well Done (Supporting)	Jeff Bainbridge	Blue Gradient Productions
The Elephant Danced (Supporting)	Jacque	Robert Anthony Hubbell Productions
The End (Lead)	John	Montoya Productions
Something Blue	Photographer	Sliding Down Rainbows Productions
The Poet (Lead)	Walter T. Elliot	Montoya Productions

Keep the columns left-justified and spaced equally. Just as with any regular job resume, the more professional it appears, the more likely those that are reading it will take you seriously. Spell check! And then spell check again - with your own eyes (not just with the computer's spell check). And do so slowly! Some people (casting directors, directors) are sticklers for proper spelling and grammar and if you have typos, you're highly likely to have your headshot tossed into file 13 (aka, the garbage can).

You'll notice that I have placed the words "Supporting", or "Lead" in parenthesis next to some of my projects. This helps tell people looking at my resume that the character I played had a lot of value in the production and sub-consciously, or consciously, lets them know I've been important and talented enough to be selected to play important parts. It gives the recipients a little more information to help in their decision making process by letting them know I can be trusted to play quality lead or supporting roles and they shouldn't have any qualms recommending me for major types of roles they're casting. So, my thoughts are, why not give a recipient a little more information to play with that reflects a positive light on my acting skills? More information is always better and it doesn't detract from how the resume looks aesthetically.

2) **T.V.**: T.V. credits differ from film. In the second column, instead of character names, you write (in order of importance):

- Lead
- Recurring
- Guest Star
- Co-Star
- Under Five

Sorry, and I know this sucks; NO extra work should be listed here. Or anywhere on your resume. Although some people will pad their resumes with extra work listings, the industry does not recognize extra work as being legitimate credits. Therefore, if you cannot list the five type of credits listed above, the more professional the person reading your resume, the more they may become suspect at your credits. For your example, your T.V. credits should be stated as thus:

Television:

| Spike TV 1000 Ways to Die | Lead | MTV Networks |
| The Last Resort (Pilot) | Co-Star | Lee Michael Cohn |

3) **New Media**: New Media includes all your internet credits. Any web series, webisodes (online short films), webisoaps, self-documentary stuff is all placed here. New Media also shares the same listing format as T.V.

New Media:

| Young Gentlemen Explorers Web Series | Lead | Standard Issue TV |
| Intern Sushi Web Series | Co-Star | InternSushi.com |

4) **Industrial**: Any type of industrial or in-house video is placed here. If you did a spot for a company, but the spot is only used in-house (i.e.. as a training, recruitment, in-store used video), it gets placed here. The format is similar now to the "Film" listings.

First, list the company name, second, your role, and third, the production house or director.

Industrial:

The Laser Center	Eye Patient	San Diego Video & Film
The Lens Shop.Com (Lead)	Action Guy	Cravin Entertainment
Strength & Muscle Fitness Video (Lead)	Fitness Coach	Overbay Productions
TCI Cablevision (Lead)	Cableman	TCI Productions

5) **Theatre**: Here's where many of you will shine. All plays you've done are listed here. The format is the same as film.

First, list the company name, second your role, and third, the theatre or production house.

Theatre:

A Few Good Men	Lt. JG Daniel Kaffee	The Actors Institute, NY, NY
Orphans	Phillip	The Actors Institute, NY, NY
The Caine Mutiny Court-Martial	Lt. Barney Greenwald	The Actors Institute, NY, NY
The Rainmaker	Noah	Actors Theater of Houston, TX
Aida	Egyptian Slave	Wortham Theater, Houston, TX

6) **Training**: All of your training goes here. List your training in order of occurrence, from current (top) to oldest (bottom).

The format is loose here. You may list the company, theatre group, workshop name, or instructor name first, and then the location. Name recognition is important in this town so if you list the principal person's name you train with first, it can't hurt for instant brownie points with the person who's reading your resume. On the other hand, sometimes the school you train with will garner higher name recognition. In that case (e.g. "Upright Citizens Brigade" – One of the best improv schools in LA), you would list the school's name first and then your instructor.

In the example below, Tom Ardavany is a well-established acting coach in LA. Melissa Skoff is a well-established and highly regarded casting director who also teaches workshops.

Tom Ardavany's, The Approach, Los Angeles, CA
Melissa Skoff's Cold Reading & Scene Study Workshop, Los Angeles, CA
Screen Acting Development, NIDA, Sydney, Australia
Screen Studies, NIDA, Sydney, Australia
Acting Intensive, NIDA, Sydney, Australia
The Actors Institute, New York, NY

As for the aesthetics of your resume, you have a little leeway as far as what font style and size you choose to create with. Just be sure to make it consistent, spaced properly and easily readable.

7) **Special Skills**: Next, you list your special skills. A special skill is defined as something you do extremely well and/or have been trained to do. For example, if you list you are a football player, then you are expected to have (at minimum) high school experience. Better yet, college or pro experience. If you speak a foreign language, you have to be fluent in that language or have notated, "conversational". The reason is if you list a foreign language and you're only conversationally fluent, you may find yourself on set with only people that speak that other language. Seriously. You, as the actor, will be expected to be able to understand whatever direction they are giving you and be able to converse freely about such. If you cannot understand what it is they're asking you to do, you're going to be in a mess of trouble.

Special Abilities:
Proficient Russian Language, Platform Speaker, Professional Flight Attendant, Professional Photographer, Stick Shift Driver (Right & Left Hand Drive) Triathlete, Fire-walker (Barefoot walking over hot coals)

Remember, time is money on a set, and if you're costing the director and producers time due to your lack of language skills, you're also costing them money and they don't like this. It will reflect badly upon you and also reflect badly on the casting director who will, without a doubt, get back to your agent about your not being honest about your skills. From that point on, you'll probably never work with these people again. Special skills should be limited to a maximum of 5 – 7 listed skills.

8) **Dialects:** Finally, list any dialects you can do well. Again, the key word here is "well". If you're able to do an English accent, then you have to be almost a natural at it. Same for any other language or regional accent you advertise.

Dialects:
Russian, Midwestern U.S., Southern U.S.

Photos and short films available for viewing via: http://www.tomgurnee.com

Finally, I've never heard of anyone having a problem with listing your personal acting website and/or IMDB link at the bottom of your resume. If you have the space available, this may help to bulk up or add to your resume.

Obviously, as your resume grows, you'll need to tailor what and how much information you incorporate into it. You may need to drop your font size down to fit more information. Whatever feels, still looks professional, is easy to read and is genuine is what matters most.

Attaching Your Resume to Your Headshot: Once you have your resume ready, print it out and cut it to the appropriate size (slightly less than 8x10) for attaching to the back of your headshot. Attaching is easy, just use a stapler and staple your resume at each top and each bottom corner. Make sure your resume is flush against your headshot while you do this; you don't want a bubble of air under your resume that will result in your resume later creasing the first time someone puts something heavy on top of it. Also, make sure your staple does not inadvertently cover any of your contact information.

All in all, your resume, to industry standard, should look something similar to this:

Tom Gurnee
(SAG Eligible)

Height: 5' 10"
Weight: 150
Hair: Brown
Eyes: Hazel

Phone: 310-123-4567
Email:
contact@movingtolaforacting.com

Film:

KingBreaker (Supporting)	Frank (The Bomber)	Matt Snead Productions
Well Done (Supporting)	Jeff Bainbridge	Blue Gradient Productions
The Elephant Danced (Supporting)	Jacque	Robert Anthony Hubbell Productions
The End (Lead)	John	Montoya Productions
Something Blue	Photographer	Sliding Down Rainbows Productions
The Poet (Lead)	Walter T. Elliot	Montoya Productions
Rear View (Lead)	Tony	Reimers Productions
Le Mistral (Lead)	Thad	KS Productions
The Last Hit	Syndicate Member #1	MMK Productions
Last Hand (Lead)	Boss	Wagner/Johnson Productions

Television:

Spike TV 1000 Ways to Die	Lead	MTV Networks
The Last Resort (Pilot)	Co-Star	Lee Michael Cohn
Wealth TV	On-Air Personality	Herring Broadcasting, Inc
TV Series The Lyons Den	Under Five	20th Century Fox Television

New Media:

Young Gentlemen Explorers Web Series	Lead	Standard Issue TV
Intern Sushi	Co-Star	Intern Sushi.com

Industrial:

The Laser Center	Eye Patient	San Diego Video & Film
The Lens Shop.Com (Lead)	Action Guy	Cravin Entertainment
Strength & Muscle Fitness Video (Lead)	Fitness Coach	Overbay Productions
TCI Cablevision (Lead)	Cableman	TCI Productions
United Airlines (Lead)	Flight Attendant	United Airlines, Inc
Herbalife	Military Color Guard Member	Herbalife, Inc

Theater:

A Few Good Men	Lt. JG Daniel Kaffee	The Actors Institute, NY, NY
Orphans	Phillip	The Actors Institute, NY, NY
The Caine Mutiny Court-Martial	Lt. Barney Greenwald	The Actors Institute, NY, NY
The Rainmaker	Noah	Actors Theater of Houston, TX
Aida	Egyptian Slave	Wortham Theater, Houston, TX

Training:
Tom Ardavany's, The Approach, Los Angeles, CA
Melissa Skoff's Cold Reading & Scene Study Workshop, Los Angeles, CA
Screen Acting Development, NIDA, Sydney, Australia
Screen Studies, NIDA, Sydney, Australia
Acting Intensive, NIDA, Sydney, Australia
The Actors Institute, New York, NY

Special Abilities:
Proficient Russian Language, Platform Speaker, Professional Flight Attendant, Professional Photographer, Stick Shift Driver (Right & Left Hand Drive), Triathlete, Fire-Walker (Barefoot walker over hot coals)

Dialects:
Russian, Midwestern U.S., Southern U.S.

Photos and short films available for viewing via: http://www.tomgurnee.com

69

Get a Reel Going

In LA, this day and age, having a reel of your work gives you an immediate leg up on your competition. Reels are small snippets of your filmed acting work that are pieced together into a montage that can last roughly up to 3-5 minutes. The purpose of a reel is to show agents and/or casting directors that you know how to act. First and foremost, you want to include any work that the widest viewing audience possible has seen and then add from there. For example, if you've done work on a television show or, if you've done work with a well-known television or film actor, you would want that to go first on your reel. Whatever or whoever is immediately recognizable gets priority. Why? This establishes instant credibility that you indeed know how to act (you got the role on that TV show or film didn't you?) and, it means you're trustworthy and know how to act professionally on set.

On your reel, you want to include varied roles that best show your acting range capabilities. That is, there should be something dramatic, something comedic, and something in-between. Show different characters. The more range and talent an agent can see, the better.

Here's the caveat though. As I just said, you want 3 – 5 things on your reel so that an agent you're looking to work with can see your talent range. The more information they have to work with the better so they know what they can send you out for. On the other hand, casting directors looking to book a role will not view your entire demo reel because they literally do not have the time. What typically happens is, if a casting director takes a quick peek at your reel, they'll know in about 10 seconds whether you can act or not. After those 10 seconds, they're either placing you in the keep category or they're moving on to the next actor.

Another (very) important reason you need a reel is for the actor's job bulletin board, Actors Access. I'll get more into what these folks do in a later section but be sure to go to and read this section thoroughly and understand how having a reel is vitally important to your submissions process for this bulletin board.

In making your reel, brevity is your best friend as far as your clips are concerned. Each clip should be around 30 seconds and certainly no longer than 60 seconds. Less (30 seconds), is more. Again, if a person can tell if you can act or not in about 10 seconds, there's not much need to exploit or overkill someone who's watching your reel with anything too much.

When "cutting" your scenes for your reel, always begin the scene with you as the major character. You should be the first person someone looking at your reel sees and the first person that speaks. Do not use "lead in" type scenes. That is, if someone or something is accosting your character in your scene before you do your thing, it doesn't matter. Cut it and leave it out. There's no need to have something "tell the story". SO many actors do this on their reels! Don't! Time spent having your viewer decide what's going on, immediately detracts from you (the star) and it tells your viewer you don't know what you're doing. Also, don't confuse your viewer by having them see someone else first. Really, why would you want a casting director or director focused on someone else? Again, the casting director is only going to watch 10 seconds(!) of your clip so don't waste this time by having them focus on something or someone other than you.

Costs: Costs in making your reel vary widely and here's where you can save some money. Unlike your headshot photographer, the best way to get a reel for yourself is to have a friend that knows Final Cut Pro (or any other good video editing software) well and have him/her do it for you. Fortunately, there aren't any real industry standards that you have to maintain here (other than what I mention in this section), so you have levity on how your reel turns out. Obviously, this is where having a buddy pays off. The only real concerns you should have are visibility (that is, make sure your video is bright enough to see) and image quality (no off-looking colors that are not intended to be there). And, of course, make sure they cut in directly onto you for your scenes. It's recommended that you label your reel at the beginning before your clips start with your name and if you are union eligible. This title page should not be longer than 5 seconds. Three seconds is about right unless you have a unique first or last name that takes someone's brain an extra moment to understand. I've seen title pages last as long as 10 seconds and all I can do to keep from pulling my hair out is wonder what the heck were they thinking.

There are services, of course, that create reels for actors and most of them will do good work for you. Google search, "actor demo reel rates" and a whole host of companies comes up. Also, check out information regarding this subject on YouTube. There are some good videos there that take you through the process and provide information on how much these services charge.

If you're looking for reel examples other than those by the companies, go to the home page on Actors Access (www.actorsaccess.com). They always have four actors they randomly profile there. Click on any of these actors and watch their reels. Get a feel for what impresses you and what turns you off, make notes, and go from there.

Training

Training, training, training. Or, as the saying goes, "Practice, practice, practice." The good news is, you're moving to one of the best towns in the world for acting training. The bad news is, you have to filter out those trainers that are real versus those that are not.

Here in Los Angeles, we have some of the finest and most reputable acting trainers in the world. We have some of the finest schools that teach with great credibility all the famous styles of acting including Miesner, Strasberg, Stanislavsky, Shakespeare… You can find many different theories, techniques and practices in many different places. Your assignment is to find acting classes that you feel comfortable in and that resonate deeply and firmly inside of you. Because it's you, after all, that is the one going in front of the camera. And you obviously want to put your best foot forward every time.

Putting your best foot forward in anything you do requires practice. Constant practice. If you do not have the discipline (or funds) to be able to continue your training in one form or another, you fall behind all of your counterparts that are able to commit. Any successful actor you run into will tell you their time in class has meant the difference between success and failure. Therefore, if you're not in class, someone else is learning that one, little technique that may mean the difference between getting the role and not getting the role. Remember the story of the oak? Get in class and stay there.

Finding a class that you feel you're a good fit for can be a bit taxing at first. You may find yourself going from school to school, class to class. But here's the good part. Many of these places allow you to audit your first class for free. If they don't, then simply move on or have a real one on one discussion with the instructor about their training regimen. Consider yourself interviewing them, just like you did with your photographer. You want to see how you get along with these people and if you'll be a good fit. Some instructors only do private coaching. Be a little cautious with these. I'm not saying they're bad, just do your due diligence. They should either have a laundry list of successful, "working" actors they've worked with or they should have excellent references and have these references available to you. Private coaching runs around $75 - $200/hour and without doing your homework, you won't be sure what you're going to get.

So, all in all, if you put yourself in a positive frame of mind towards exploring all of the available and different possibilities, you might find that going from class to class can be fun. Just think of all the different notes and techniques you'll have and see…

Rates: Once you do find a school or teacher you're comfortable with, chances are the rates are going to be in the $250 - $300/month range. (Write this into your spreadsheet!) Some schools like to ask for payment for two months in advance with a little discount for doing so, others will simply go month-to-month. Payment is expected to be rendered the first class of the month and typically, if you have to miss a class for whatever reason, you are not given a rebate or makeup class. Some instructors are flexible on this rule (i.e., they allow missing class if you book a job), but be sure you clarify what the rules are concerning attendance before you commit to the class. You don't want to be surprised and end up having negative thoughts about an instructor (which will inhibit the creative process when you take a class) when/if an awkward situation presents itself.

Another good idea is to get as much feedback on a school and/or instructor as you can before you commit. Look in different places to solicit this information and try to get it as unbiased as possible. Also, consider your personal temperament. Are you a good match for an instructor that's going to be a real and serious hard ass on you? Are you seriously ok with a teacher saying to you and meaning it, "What the fuck was that?" Teachers are humans too, and they all have their own styles. Some will coddle you, some will play it straight with you, some will rip you a new one. It's up to you to determine what style of teaching they incorporate that will not trample upon your values as a human being but will at the same time be challenging enough to where you have to work to gain their respect.

Another question to ask your prospective instructor is do they do showcases? Showcases are excellent ways to show off your talent directly to people in the industry that are invited to come and see you.

74

Ask questions regarding how many classes does one take before the instructor allows or thinks one is ready to be showcased. Ask about how many industry people typically show up to the showcases? Who are these people? Are they agents, managers and/or directors with a who's who Rolodex of who they can send you to? Or are these folks a little bit more down the food chain on having decision making powers? Who are some of the regulars? Look these people up on IMDBPRO and find out if they're legit! Showcases can be helpful with garnering you an agent or small role so keep them in mind when looking around for a school and/or acting instructor.

IMPROV: All casting directors, agents, managers and directors will tell you improvisational training is a big plus to have on your resume. The top three Improv schools in LA are (in no particular order):

- UCB ~ Upright Citizens Brigade (http://losangeles.ucbtrainingcenter.com)
- Groundlings (http://www.groundlings.com/school/getting-started.aspx) and
- Second City (http://www.secondcity.com/training/)

Having one of these schools on your resume is like having a little gold star on it. Casting directors really like seeing these schools (ding, ding, name recognition again!), because they know they're reputable, they give excellent training and they know these schools train you to think on your feet. Basically, it tells them you're a serious actor. As for these schools, unfortunately they do not allow auditing and you may be required to audition to be accepted. Check out their websites and do your due diligence by checking out their FAQ sections. Call them up and have a nice chat with the receptionist about what it is you're looking for, as well as what it is they require you to do before entering into their space.

Keep in mind, while improv is an excellent skill to have, it does not substitute for all the basics of acting. There's actually a new wave of sentiment out there that says agents should not be ringing the improv bell so hard for perspective clients. This is because a lot of actors these days are shorting their acting foundations in lieu of taking short

75

cuts. If you don't have the basics down, you sell yourself short and it will show on camera and perhaps, stunt your career. Again, get yourself into a reputable acting class, stay there, learn and firm up your foundation and add to and enhance those skills by taking improv.

Extra Work

For those of you who don't know what an "extra" is, here's a brief description of who they are and where you see (or don't see) them. The scene is a courthouse. Two lead actors are playing lawyers and they're walking down a hallway towards a courtroom speaking to each other. They pass people and police officers in the hallway and they pass people seated in the courtroom they enter. These people who aren't saying anything the actors are passing are known as "extras".

Extras (otherwise known as "background" actors) are non-speaking role actors that are used to "fill-up" a scene and/or to help give it life. There can be as few as one person used as an extra for a scene or as many as hundreds or even thousands. Sometimes an extra can be very prominent in the scene (meaning they are working very close to or with a speaking-role actor) or they are unfocused, color blobs walking in the distant background. The main thing is, no matter where you end up working, you're getting paid.

Many people poo-poo the idea of being an extra but if you're new to L.A. and are looking to get your feet wet, I personally think being an extra is a great way to start. The main and most important reason is it gets you on the set. You're right where you dream of being and now you have the opportunity to take it all in. You get to see all of the dynamics of how a set works and operates. You get to see how the behind-the-scenes crew interact with each other, as well as with the director, and you get to see how scenes are created from start to finish. You get to see how the director interacts with the actors and crew and how the leading actors themselves prepare and rehearse. It's all happening right in front of you and all you have to do is: whatever it is you're assigned to do! Take advantage of this great opportunity you have by consciously observing how everyone works each other and what all the nuances are that come with the territory. Learn the phrasing people are using on set, learn the hierarchy of who is who and what responsibilities they have. Watch how it all unfolds and you'll learn first-hand how movies and television are made.

Typically, extras don't have intricate assignments. In the years I worked as an extra, most of what I did/observed were assignments that consisted of walking from point A to B in the background of a scene. Othertimes, I was a patron at a restaurant or café and seated, miming words with someone else who was seated near me when the camera was near. In other words, don't expect very much in regards to camera time because the simple fact is, you're not there to get camera time (hence the reason you're called "background"). You're only – and most of the time – primary job is to be a filler of some sort.

Extra work can be exceedingly fun, and exceedingly boring. As for the boring part, suffice it to say the Army has nothing on the phrase, "Hurry up and wait". You can expect to be quickly shuffled to a holding area that has a few chairs and four walls. You can expect to be quickly shuffled from there to set and then asked to wait some more. After your assigned task, you'll be briskly shuffled back to holding again where you could potentially wait for hours (yes, hours) before you're called again.

As for the fun part, you never know what's going to happen. You'll be asked to take part in a scene and be given your task right there on the spot. If you're really lucky, one of the associate directors will choose you out of the extras group and have what is called a "feature" task for you. That is, you'll be working directly or very close to one of the stars. I instantly became Rob Lowe's personal waiter for a scene because I had a look the director thought was right. All I had to do was walk up with a serving tray, place down two glasses and a pitcher of water in front of Rob Lowe and not spill anything. Fortunately, I did my job well and after the scene was over Rob came to me and said, "Good job!" (The pitcher of water was quite large and heavy!)

Instances like this are rare, but they do happen. What's nice is when they do, besides this wonderful opportunity you just had, you're sometimes given a "bump" in pay rate as a "featured extra" versus being a regular one. It's told that directors sometimes will give an extra a very small speaking line for the scene. These are extremely rare because it means a huge headache is about to hit the line producer, but they do happen. When it does, if you were on a SAG set, you just got a first-class invitation to get a SAG card without going through all the hoops. Don't get your hopes up that you're going to show up on set and the director is going to see and instantly fall in love with you – 9,999 times out of 10,000 this just won't happen. But, I will say again, "you never know" when you put your intention out there that something positive will happen for you.

An extra is the lowest of the low on the totem pole on a set and unfortunately some crew will take liberty of this and be overly bossy with their attitudes towards you. Most of the time you will be treated with respect and it's your job to return the favor and not be disrespectful to anyone you meet. Feel free to meet crew members when they're not working and if you're lucky, network with them. Crew members can sometimes turn into fast-track friends that can refer you for future work.

Pay is pretty good…if you're a SAG union extra. Pay if you're a non-union extra? Hahaha! Yes, the joke's on you. Eight to ten bucks an hour or whatever the minimum is they can get away with legally. That's right, there's quite the discrepancy. Hence, if you're coming in from out of state and are already a union actor, a super way to instantly supplement your income is to be an extra out here. Union extra actors make a minimum of $324/day. Not too shabby for being asked to do relatively nothing on set. Non-union actors; you're the suckers and can expect $64/8 hours. Both union and non-union actors begin making time and a half after 8 hours of work (one hour taken for lunch is not included in this) and both begin making double-time every hour after 12 hours.

What else can you expect? Well, besides what I'm writing there's a lot to be said here. Brad Hall, a contributing writer to the industry job board "EntertainmentCareers.net" has a good explanation. You can read it here:

http://www.entertainmentcareers.net/acting/becoming_and_extra.asp

Regarding time, one thing to expect is to stay on set all 8 hours. You can expect to wait around a lot of those hours. Even if they don't need you, you'll be asked to stick around "just in case". If you go into overtime, you probably won't be there too much longer. Only twice have I ever gone into double overtime. And trust me, you really don't want to go into double overtime. It's taxing enough on your body to wait around in a confined space for more than 8 hours much less 12 or more.

A few rules to remember when working as an extra:

Never, ever ask for an autograph from one of the stars. This is the fastest way to being asked to leave.

Do not initiate conversations with the stars. This is the second fastest way of being asked to leave. If a star or working actor initiates conversation with you, you may answer. Be brief and enjoy it while it lasts, but never try to start a dialog.

Go to the bathroom every chance you get. Your holding area may not be equipped or have a bathroom nearby and when you're asked to be close-by to come on set, you absolutely do not want to be the singular cause production is being held up.

Bring a book (or make sure your phone is charged up and you have something to read on it).

"If" (and that's a big if) a set allows you to bring your phone onto it, be absolutely sure it is set to silent. Typically, do not expect your being allowed to bring it to or near set because these days phones can actually interfere with wireless camera signals. You're usually ok to have it in your holding area, but just know that when you leave to go to set, it has to stay behind.

If you're on set and the crew breaks for lunch, good for you! Usually, the food is quite good. However, since you are last on the totem pole you will be last to have the opportunity to eat. Crew and actors go first, then you. Don't worry though, they typically do not run out of food when you get up to give your order.

Keep your voices down in the holding room. A fast way to get on an associate director's bad side is to have them constantly come and bug you about being too loud.

If you bring your computer, be mentally prepared to lose it if it should it somehow sprout legs and walk away while you're on set (especially towards the end of day). As much as we all would like to think everyone is honorable and trustworthy on set, alas, sometimes it just isn't so.

WHERE TO FIND EXTRA WORK:

The largest and best extra casting agency is Central Casting (www.centralcasting.com). They're located up in Burbank and are the industry leaders when it comes to extra casting, casting around 2,000 people/day. They take all types and you'll see all different types if/when you go to register. They have very specific registration days/times and a LOT of information to digest before you sign up so go to their website and read everything there is about the agency and what you have to do before arriving. Registration fee is $25 cash only (bring correct change) and be absolutely sure to bring all of the personal identification documentation they need to complete registration for you. One final note, be sure to know all of your sizing information and bring a couple extra pictures with you to denote they type of characters you're willing to play.

Other noted extra agencies out there include:

www.creativeextrascasting.com

www.extraextracasting.com

www.billdancecasting.com

www.backtoonecasting.com

There are other extra sites out there to peruse. Do a Google search for "extra casting Los Angeles" or something similar and search what comes up. Be advised, some of these agencies are pay-to-play organizations, meaning some will charge you an upfront fee (one-time), a monthly fee or no fee at all and only take a percentage of what you make from your check. You can typically expect to pay something for signing up but never pay more than $100 to register for anyone. Also, be prepared to talk about your wardrobe in detail and do NOT sign up with anyone that does not ask you about your wardrobe or your special skills and talents. After that, it's up to you how much or how little you would like to work in this town and for whom. Always do your due diligence regarding any outfit you choose to sign up with!

Workshops

Another, yet weaker form of training is doing workshops. Workshops are usually taught by casting directors, casting associates and talent managers. Typically, these workshops run from 1 – 4 weeks (one day per week) in length and they are decent ways to establish relationships with these people who are in positions to give you advice regarding your acting and career.

Workshops will vary widely in subject matter. For example, you can take workshops on comedy, soaps, commercials, theatrical training, auditioning, learning the business, etc, etc. It's up to you to decide what you think is important to know right now and/or with whom you want to try to begin an upfront professional relationship with.

Workshops are 50/50 with actors. Some people love them, believing they are great ways to get to know what it is casting directors, for example, are looking for. They think they're great ways to get face-to-face with those they could respectively be seeing in auditions. On the other hand, other actors think they're a huge scam. They'll tell you they are simply ways casting associates and casting directors siphon money from wannabe actors and they'll be quick to tell you that of all the people they see, statistics say they'll only ask 1.5 – 3% of those students to come in for auditions. That is approximately the same percentage of auditions an actor secures using bulletin board casting websites.

I think what's important to remember here is most of the people teaching these courses have been working in their respective positions for years. Taking one or two classes could potentially have positive returns for you. If you take a workshop, what you must remember is, these people are in absolutely no way obligated to give you any sort of job, much less an audition. A lot of actors go into workshops believing the person instructing will immediately give them an audition, but that's not the case. What most tend to say is that yes, they do give auditions to those people who attend their classes, but what they don't tell you is the number of people they see coming from workshops is very small.

From the workshops I have attended, I have found them all to be relatively worthwhile substantively and decent enough for networking. Remember, it's all about networking in this town and the more relationships you can begin to create the better. Obviously, before taking a workshop ask about what will be covered in the course and see if it matches your intentions on taking it.

There are a few places in LA that cater to this business. One is Actors Creative Workshop (http://www.trulyacting.com/). ACW has a huge instructor list and their calendar is always full of classes and workshops that are being given. Visit their website and then navigate to their "Classes" link and you'll see what is available. ACW also puts on "free" one-hour classes with several of these instructors. These so-called "classes" are indeed free, but they're mostly glorified sales-pitches. That being said, most of these incorporate time for Q&A into these free meetings so you gain a lot of information on things you want to learn if you're prepared to do so. Some of these one-hour classes will have audience participation; meaning they'll ask for volunteers to do a little on-camera work, but keep in mind they're doing this mostly to show you what you'll be working on in their class vs. actually teaching you something right there on the spot. All in all, I do recommend these one-hour free classes because it puts a face to the name and you never know what little gem will come out of their mouths that will help you in your career.

Another workshop space is The Casting Network: (http://www.castingnetwork.net/) Before gaining admission into their space, actors are required to audition. You'll be given a script to cold read and paired with another actor to work. You have 10 – 20 minutes to prepare and then off you go in front of all the actors who are there in attendance with you. In short, they're looking to see how you handle yourself in cold read situations by how you relate to your partner and what kind of choices you make. After you audition, you will (or will not) be sent an invitation to join their workshops. If you do gain admittance, workshops with different casting directors, agents, directors, etc, are available to purchase.

"Actors West!" (http://www.actorswest.com) is yet another workshop space. Besides casting director and agent workshops, they offer a variety of acting classes that teach audition skills, cold reading, improv, etc. From what I have seen on their website, they usually have a full calendar and a few discounts on their pricing so check them out.

"The Actor's Key" (www.actorskey.com) has a very nice facility in Burbank. Many of their casting directors are top notch and they advertise their clients on their homepage (which is free advertising for you!). For whatever reason (i.e., "Due to new regulations" – whatever that means), they charge an annual fee of $12 to become a member. They have a relatively generous cancellation policy; on the yearly membership, that is, you have 10 days and on any class, if you're able to cancel within 48 hours you get credit for another class. Or, if you have to cancel within the last 48 hours, you may receive credit if another late student comes in and takes your place. The only real thing to be very careful of is their parking situation which is clearly defined on their website.

"The Hollywood Acting Workshop" (www.hollywoodactingworkshop.com) is a no membership fee outfit that offers beginning, intermediate and advanced television, film and commercial classes on top of offering casting director workshops. Four week class workshops are $200. They also offer "5 Agent" and "5 Manager" showcases on a weekly basis that run $89 - $99 in price. If you sign up on their email list, they will send you a monthly schedule that includes the workshops they offer.

What's different is, they include the names of the professionals (the agents/managers) that will be attending and the outfits they work for. That way, you can see if you match up as an actor with their agencies or companies. On Thursday evenings from 7pm – 10pm, they allow you to audit a four-week scene study class which is cool, but you have to register in advance through their website and answer some goofy questions like, "Are you currently able to pay $200 to attend a 4-week session of this class?" and "Is the West Hollywood locaation a managable drive for you on Thursday nights?" I'll let you decide what you think about these and how you'd respond to them…

"Actors Alley Workshops" (www.actorsalleyworkshops.com) is yet another resource that offers acting workshops and classes given by casting directors and agents. These guys are in Van Nuys so if you end up living in the Valley, they may be a closer venue for you to visit. Their website is a bit drab and a little sketchy to navigate at first but when you get use to it, it's reasonably logical to work through. Here's a hint to save some time, when you go to the homepage, click the button to the right of the Actors Alley Workshops logo (it has three white lines on top of each other). This will show the site navigation links for you. Actors Alley Workshops offers four to six week classes on different areas of acting and are offered at $200. Lastly, if you choose to sign up for their emails, be prepared to be blitzed with them once a day or every other day regarding their calendar of events.

Rates: Rates overall on workshops vary but they run more or less in the $50/day range. I have seen one day workshops run from $35 - $65, two day workshops from $65 - $100, four day workshops around the $225 level and six day workshops around $300. Sometimes these people and places have sales (i.e., I did a 4 day workshop with a top talent manager for $165) so be sure to get on their email lists.

Finally, please keep in mind, when I say 2 "day", or 4 "day" workshops, this means you attend one class per week. For example, if you attend a "4-day" workshop that takes place on Tuesdays, you will be attending four, separate and individual Tuesday evening classes over a month's time.

Casting Directors vs. Producers/Directors

Now that I've mentioned a little bit about workshops, I briefly want to explain a little about the food chain here in Hollywood. Consider this just a little tid-bit to keep in the back of your mind when you choose to do workshops, do mailings, go to network parties, etc.

In Hollywood, there's a pecking order concerning who has the authority to give you work. That is, when you audition, do you really know who's making the decisions regarding who says yes to you, and who does not? Well, here's your brief lesson.

At the top of the pecking list are the producers and the directors. Producers are the ones who bring in the money to fund projects and when they have the notion to cast someone in their project, typically everyone else involved in the making of the picture listens up. Obviously, one does not want to piss off a producer that's bringing several million dollars into the project for fear of them yanking their investor and his or her money along with it. Fortunately though, producers are typically very intelligent people and they don't get in the way (too much) of the hiring (casting) process.

While the producers are at the top of the tier, it mostly falls to the director of the project to make the yes or no calls on who gets cast. That means yes, it's the directors themselves, not the casting directors that make the decisions to cast you.

A casting director's job, in a nutshell, is to find those actors who they think are right for the role that's being offered and present them to the director. A casting director's reputation and future work in this town resides on bringing actors to the director that they, not just think, but know, will do a great job in the role. I'll talk about this more later on, but after whittling 750 or so actors down to 30-50 that have submitted for a role they (the casting director) put out, the casting director will have their first auditions. After these first auditions, the CD will whittle the 30-50 down to 10-20 and have call-backs (a second audition for the same role). After the call-backs, the CD typically will whittle it down to about 5 actors and present these tapes to the director, who will then decide who to award the role to.

So, to be clear, a casting director's job is to be a filter. Their job is <u>not</u> to hire, but to filter, <u>for the director</u>, those actors who come in vying for the job. It's the director of the project that actually hires you.

Why is this important to know? To potentially save you money. You're going to be doing a lot of mailing when you get here, aren't you? So the question is, are you going to be mailing your headshots, postcards and letters to the right people <u>that are the actual decision makers</u>?

Think about it.

Mailing a headshot and cover letter today costs $1.15. Do you want to spend $1.15 mailing to someone who may or may not call you into a project? Or, do you want to mail to someone that does have the authority to call you in for an audition? It's a choice you have to make for yourself.

If you do choose to mail direct to the decision makers, there are a couple of resources you can utilize to find contact information for them. First is, www.IMDBPRO.com. I'll be talking a bit more about IMDB and its paid site twin, IMDBPRO.com in a little bit.

One former way people used to reach the decision makers was via the <u>Hollywood Creative Directory</u>. The HCD was a bible of production houses that ranged from small to huge and the information contained within was gold. Unfortunately, in 2013, the parent company for this publication was bought by an outsider that quickly squashed the directory, putting it out of print. You can find old publications around various shops in LA or online and the prices vary. Keep in mind, while the information within use to be updated every quarter every year it was published, now that it's out of print, that information will be old. Some production houses may still be around, some may not.

Why utilize this publication? Because it listed: all the current production companies in Los Angeles, who worked/works in these companies, what they developed, what they're credited for and most importantly, it included/includes all of their contact information.

Your other resource is the Directory of Members publication from the Directors Guild of America (http://www.dga.org/). You can find this publication at the Samuel French Bookstore retailed at $30, or, you can pick it up directly at the Directors Guild of America main headquarters building (7920 Sunset Blvd, Los Angeles, CA, 90046) for $5.00 cheaper. Their phone numbers are: (310) 289-2000, (800) 421-4173.

How to utilize these resources:

After you've watched a movie that you think you would have been a qualified actor for, within that movie's credits will be the name of the director. Copy the director's name down onto your list. Once you've compiled 25 director's names, you go to the two directories and/or IMDBPRO.com and you find which directors have their own production companies. The reason you need both publications and the website is because sometimes their contact information is given in one resource (publication), but not in another. Drag, I know. But, when you do find one of your directors and their contact info is in either of the two books or online, you have a leg up on the competition.

Now comes the fun part where we see how disciplined and how patient you can be. Begin your mailings to your new friends and… don't expect anything in return. Follow through again – and don't expect anything in return. Follow through again, and again, and again (we're talking postcards by now, not headshots that you're sending out), each time mentioning something new either regarding you or regarding them and their latest project. Persistence. Persistence. Persistence. Why do this? Because you just never know when you're going to get a phone call out of the blue saying, "Hey, we'd like you to come in and audition for this…" And trust me, if the director himself is calling you into audition, you're already on Boardwalk about to pass "Go" while all the others are still only on Mediterranean Avenue.

Don't get me wrong! Casting Directors can be your friends and you want to get to know as many of them as you possibly can. They're the ones that can and will put you into the last bunch of actors that go before the directors. But, when push comes to shove, would you rather be friends with a casting director, or the actual director him on the project that has the power and authority to say, "You're in!"

Nothing in the world can take the place of Persistence. Talent will not; nothing is more common than unsuccessful men with talent. Genius will not; unrewarded genius is almost a proverb. Education will not; the world is full of educated derelicts. Persistence and determination alone are omnipotent. The slogan 'Press On' has solved and always will solve the problems of the human race.

~Calvin Coolidge – 30th President of the United States

Marketing Yourself & Networking

Marketing yourself and networking is <u>the most important work</u> you'll do for your career. And yet, so few actors are disciplined enough to do it. When it all comes down to it, people either know you're out there, or they don't. What side of the fence do you want to be on?

As I mentioned earlier, one of the most powerful ways to get started marketing yourself is building you fan base. Once again, utilize the tools online that have been created for just this very thing. Get a super friends list going on Facebook. Their imposed friends limit is 5000 so when you reach this, start up another page for yourself. Twitter; the sky's the limit. Tweet something every day and ask people to follow you. YouTube: If you can, self-produce, then by all means self-produce, self-produce. Find some like-minded people that have access to a video camera and get something going for yourself. The more hits your video(s) brings in, the better.

Another extremely important factor in marketing yourself and networking is again about establishing relationships. Because that's what you're doing. Putting yourself on people's radars and honing relationships - with producers, with directors, with casting directors, with their assistants, with everyone. I'll say it again, if no one knows who you are, then no one knows who you are. Marketing yourself is absolutely crucial to this game of becoming a working actor and you absolutely must be diligent and dedicated to doing it on an absolute, consistent basis.

<u>Where to begin</u>. Remember your financial spreadsheet you have going for yourself? It's time to create a new one called, "Contacts". Please do this now – go into Excel (or, what ever spreadsheet software you're utilizing) and make a new file called "Contacts". In this file, create the following headings for individual columns across a single line:

- Name
- Title
- Phone
- Email

- Office address
- Date of Initial Contact
- Place of Initial Contact
- Notes
- Mailing Dates
- Mailing Notes

Every, single, time you meet someone in the industry who has some sort of clout (Producer, Director, CD, Talent Agent), fill in the blanks of your spreadsheet.

For example, you attend a workshop with Casting Director, Joe Smith. Record down everything you can regarding him and the workshop. Enter this info into your records. Their name, their title, their phone (most will give you their office phone numbers if you attend their classes), their emails, the date of the class and where it was held and any and all notes you gathered while in class. Write down everything you can – meaning where/how did they get their start? How did they end up in LA? What was their first job? How did they end up where they are now? What are their likes, dislikes, personal tastes, do they like receiving mail, if so, what kind, how often? What do they cast for? TV, movies, both, how often, etc, etc, etc. The more personal and professional information you have the better. Why all this information? So you can personalize and tailor your mailings to them later on.

One actress who recently found a talent manager (and subsequently a theatrical agent) to work with told us during a workshop meeting regarding the business of acting that every time she met with a potential agent, she brought in her notebook of notes with her. And she literally had a full notebook. She said she would pass this notebook to the agents for them to see and tell them, "Anytime you should find yourself submitting to any of these people, you can personalize your submission with something from this," (her notebook). Does that not make for a serious, excellent first-impression or what? Granted it took her a bit of time to build up these contacts of hers but when the time came and she felt she was ready to hit it, that's exactly what happened. She signed with the talent manager I mentioned with whom she met. He, in turn, ended up sending her to one of the best talent agents in town for her level and she successfully signed with them. Furthermore, in only three weeks after getting signed with her agent, she booked a lead role on General Hospital and has since become a lead character on the show. This girl was serious about her career, was serious about her training and was serious about her networking and it paid off in a big way. And the really great part is she was only 23.

So yes, make and record notes.

Another reason you make notes is to use them for your mailings. How many people do casting directors see a week? Dozens, if not hundreds? Think they're going to remember you quickly? Not if you weren't in one of their extended week classes they won't. Jog their memories by writing something about your encounter with them in your mailing. Where, when… Nothing extravagant and do NOT write a book. Just a little something is all you need. "Hey Joe! It's Tom from the workshop I took with you last month. I just booked a commercial for XYZ Company and thought I'd spread the good news. Hope you're well!" Begin with a note immediately after the seminar so you stay fresh in their mind. Jog their memory again a little later with where you two met and chances are they'll remember your face from your picture(s) and then remember who you are.

Types of Personalized Marketing:

Postcards: As I've alluded to, postcards are your friends. Casting agents and casting directors and just about everyone do not mind them at all. Why? The first reason is they're unobtrusive. It takes time to open a letter and if you're already inundated with mail that you have to open, plus a couple dozen headshots a day, all those little seconds begin to take up precious time. I realize it doesn't sound like much, but think about it this way. The time spent opening all this mail could be time spent by your agent pitching you on the phone for a role to a casting director. Would you rather your agent be pitching you on the phone or opening up a new headshot? That's why everyone likes postcards; they don't take up time. By sending a postcard, they immediately see your face and with the flip of a wrist, read your brief comments. Quick, easy and painless.

Postcards are still relatively inexpensive to send in the mail. As of today, the price to mail a first-class postcard (Max 6" x 4.25") is $0.34. (Warning: anything over these dimensional specs and you bump up into the next price category, which is $.047.) Postcards are cheaper than sending headshots, which cost around $1.15 to send (not including the price of the mailing envelope). Hence, you get more bang for your buck (roughly 4 postcards per 1 headshot) and can cover more territory.

Plan on sending some things out? Good. Jot down in your spreadsheet the funds you'll be appropriating to:

> the number of postcards sent x $0.34
> the number of headshots sent x $1.15
> the price of envelopes (9x11's run 100 typically for $10)

When addressing your postcards, some people use labels, some people handwrite. I prefer handwriting simply because I think it's more personal, but that's just me. That being said, however, <u>always handwrite your note</u>. (Neatly!) Nothing screams junk mail more than seeing typing on the back of a postcard. If your note is handwritten, it will be read. Ever get those realty postcards in the mail? Ever take time to read them? Not much I would bet. Ever get a handwritten postcard from a friend? You took the time to read it, didn't you? Same goes for your postcards to the industry folks.

Lastly, keep you notes BRIEF! Just like I wrote above. Short, sweet and to the point:

> *"Hey Joe! It's Tom from the workshop I took with you last month. I just booked a commercial for XYZ Company and thought I'd spread the good news. Hope you're well!"*

> *"Hi Jane! Just letting you know I booked a national commercial for Ford Motors today! I'd love to come in and audition with you sometime for XYZ Show! Thanks!"*

"Hi Sam! Just saw on Casting About that you're now working on XYZ show. Congratulations! Please keep me in mind for any Co-Star roles that I may be right for!"

"Hi Debbie! Just wanted to drop you a line to say I've begun training at UCB! I'm looking forward to auditioning for one of your comedy roles sometime!

Little notes like these put you on their radar. With a few (or many) more follow-ups, you may actually get a phone call. Again, don't write a book. If you do, you lessen the chance of your postcard being read and increase the chance it goes straight into the garbage. Besides, there isn't really a lot of space on a postcard to write and if you cram a lot of tiny, hand-written text onto the back of a postcard, you're going to annoy the casting director who can't read very well without their glasses. Just keep it simple.

Vistaprint: To print your postcards (or business cards, or a whole bunch of other stuff), one place to try is Vistaprint (www.vistaprint.com). Vistaprint is one of the larger online printer outfits and they got this way by having low prices, having decent quality and offering crazy discounts. Vistaprint company is a perfect example of, if you do good work for people, word of mouth does the rest for you. Here's an example: how does 100 free postcards sound? No joke. Vistaprint will at times advertise deals such as 100 free postcards and 250 free business cards. The fine print is you just pay a little extra for the shipping charges (I.e., $6.95 for the postcards, $7.05 for business cards).

These sales unfortunately, come and go. So when you see them, you have to jump on them because they don't stick around for very long.

One way I was able to access their free sale was by "liking" them on Facebook. Sometimes this approach works, sometimes it does not. That is, it worked once for one of my Facebook profiles, but it did not for another. At any rate, it's worth a shot when you're ready to print postcards for yourself.

Here's what you do. First, go to Facebook and "like" Vistaprint. (https://www.facebook.com/vistaprint). After this, you'll see an instant discount in their retail pricing. Next, visit their website and create an account for yourself. Navigate to the postcards link and experiment with how the uploading and designing features work. Don't worry; you won't have to pay unless you're actually ready to print something at the end. Be sure to make the postcard link the first product link you check out. Why? Because most of the advertisements you'll hopefully begin to see popping up after that will be for the free postcards (I started seeing them immediately pop up on Gmail, Yahoo and even Couponmom.com just minutes after I left Vistaprint's site).

What's happening is your computer has accepted an electronic cookie from Vistaprint and the company (and internet spiders) key in on this. (Ever noticed that after you buy something online that the advertisements you now see are now related to the product you just bought? Who says the internet is totally free from Big Brother...) Anyhow, score your free 100 postcards from one of these ads and be happy.

Now, there's only one catch and it's minor, but YOU have to rectify it. At the time of this writing, during the postcard design process, they want to print their logo on your postcards. This can be simply remedied by deleting their logo during the design process! Just click on this part of the design process and simply delete it. It's that simple.

Another place I've found on the net is PSPrint (http://www.PSPrint.com). On occasion they have some pretty stellar sales (60% off). So for a small batch of 50 postcards, glossy front, 14pt paper, color on the front, b/w on the back, for example, the job is running $18.50 with no shipping costs and has only a 3 day turnaround. That's pretty good. Full color both sides, just under $22. Again, these are sale prices that happen, so it doesn't hurt to check in on them every once and a while.

Obviously, there are other online printers you can find and use. Do your research and see if you can find a company having a sale.

If/when you find a good one that you like that has great prices, please let me know about it! I'd be happy to share your good fortune with my other readers.

Headshots/Resumes & Cover Letters: There are differing opinions on whether to enclose a cover letter with your headshot or not. For those who do not read them, they say that a sticky note on your headshot will suffice to say a couple words. For those that do, well then you want to obviously include your cover letter. How do you know which casting directors read cover letters and which do not? The only way is to ask them anytime you are in their presence, or ask their secretary should you call their office. If you don't know, use your best judgment.

When sending, if you have two different headshots, include them both. Attach a resume to the back of your headshot(s) and insert your cover letter on top of it so the cover letter is the first thing the recipient sees when they open your envelope. As for cover letters, again, be brief and to the point. Accentuate the positives (recent roles, your training, your special skills) and leave out the rest. Really, leave out the rest. Spell check! And spell check again.

During one of my workshops with a talent manager, he gave us an example of what NOT to do (write):

Dear Mr. (only gave the Talent Mgr's first name here)

I am an actor and I would like to inquire about a meeting at your office. Your agency has been recommended to me as one of most highly in the industry. I would be interested in learning more about you and about available representation.
I have had the privilege of honing my acting abilities in college, acclaimed acting studios in Los Angeles, performing plays and writing.

My resume and link to my reel, which is enclosed, contains additional information on my experience and skills. I would appreciate the opportunity to discuss representation with you and to provide further information on my readiness. Reel link http://xxxxxxxxx

Our talent manager told us he found at least 6 things wrong with this cover letter. He said something has to be pretty bad for it to become an example of what <u>not</u> to do for the class. I would hope you would agree.

Again, be specific and brief with your training, roles and special skills. Here is an example of what <u>to</u> do:

1234 Street Ave
Los Angeles, CA 90210
01 January 2012

Agent's Name
Company Name
1234 Sunset Blvd. Ste 123
Los Angeles, CA 90210

Hello Mr. Jones!

I am currently seeking representation here in Los Angeles and would appreciate your consideration.

My recent credits include a lead role on Spike TV's, "1000 Ways to Die", a national commercial for AZEK Decking and I am the lead in a new web series entitled, "Young Gentlemen Explorers", that is scheduled to premiere online this month. I am also SAG-E.

Here in Los Angeles, I train with Tom Ardavany. I have also trained in New York City at The Actors Institute and the National Institute of Dramatic Arts in Sydney, Australia.

Thank you for your consideration and please note that I speak Russian.

Best of Days,

Your Name
310-123-4567
youremail@youraddress.com
www.yourwebsite.com

Some things to notice: Simply state that you are "seeking representation". Do not state, "theatrical", or "commercial" representation. You don't need to. "…Would appreciate your consideration." No need to embellish here, either. Just simply state that you would appreciate their consideration. That's it. Keep what you have to say to the point and keep it tight. Finally, if you have an acting website, list it under your name as part of your contact info. Do not make a paragraph out of it. If they want to look at it, they will.

Finally, type your cover letter.

When sending your headshots, again use labels or handwrite (neatly) the address on the envelope. As for envelopes, do NOT use special, "see-through" envelopes that are sold online and in shops. If you've never seen one of these envelopes, they have a see-through cellophane window in front that you put your headshot directly behind and within so people can see your headshot without opening your letter. And this is exactly why you should not use them. If an agent or casting person doesn't like your look through one of these envelopes, you go straight into the trash. Seriously! You could have the most amazing cover letter, have the most amazing credits and have the greatest training, but you won't even give yourself the chance of them seeing any of these things if they don't open your letter. Don't limit yourself from the get-go. Every talent agent, manager, and casting person I've met have all said they open their mail. Every one of these people have admitted that they have trashed headshot letters (unopened!) that were sent using these envelopes because they simply didn't like their look. Give yourself the best opportunity you can right from the beginning.

One last note about these envelopes… They're expensive. They literally run about a dollar a piece. Save your money and let some other actor waste theirs.

When you seal a regular envelope you use, just seal it a little bit. In other words, there's really no need to lick the entire sealing area. I know this sounds a little ADD, but it's the little things that make a big difference sometimes. As I've mentioned, it takes time to open envelopes. If a casting director is struggling to open your envelope because it's solidly sealed, you've inadvertently caused them to have an unconcious negative impression about you and they haven't even seen your face yet. Just give your envelope a little lick in the middle; just enough of a seal to get from point A to point B. The person opening your envelope will thank you for the easy effort it took to open your letter and you'll remain a positive person in their subconscious mind.

Acting Websites: It's the Internet age people and if you don't have a website, then you're living in the Stone Age. Websites today, are the business cards of yesterday. You don't absolutely need one, but it sure helps in the marketing of yourself if you do. Remember, you're the CEO of your company and if you don't have a website advertising your wares, people are going to miss you and your product.

Your acting website is a great way to advertise yourself. You just simply throw your website link into an email and boom, you're done. You've just "marketed" yourself (provided the person on the receiving ends opens your website link, of course). But it's something that's immediate that puts you in the mind of the recipient. And the best part is it doesn't cost you anything to send it.

Creating your acting website is easy these days. Most internet providers have ways to instantly create websites and you can create a profesional looking website for yourself in very little time. Personally, I have a little bit of experience in web design and so I built my own website. My site is www.tomgurnee.com. So long as your site shows your photo(s), lists your resume and has some sort of contact information on it, you're good to go. Don't forget your reel(s)! Your acting site is the perfect place to market and show your reel(s) without having to create video cds and paying to send them to people who aren't going to look at them. (Video cds use to be one way an actor would market themselves. Instead of a full size cd, a video cd was about the size of a silver dollar. They cost about a dollar a piece to create. The only issue was/is, most people on the receiving end of these video cds did not have a cd player next to them in their office and hence, these expensive little items went into the trash. You may still find people out there that can create them for you and they'll tout how excellent they can be for your marketing, but take what they say with a large grain of salt for the main reason I just mentioned above. Instead, just send a weblink of your reel in an email or list where they can find your reel on your website and you're good to go.)

<u>What you'll need & costs</u>: First, you need to secure your domain name. Your domain name should be your name, .com. (Just like my example, www.tomgurnee.com). If you have a relatively generic name and someone else already has this domain name, then you either have the choice of securing a .net, .biz, .whatever after your name for your domain, or, you'll have to supplement your name with another word. For example, www.actorjohndoe.com. Something like this. Keep in mind, name recognition is huge and if and when you become famous, if you don't have your name already registered for yourself, you can bet your bottom dollar someone else will buy your name and build a who-knows-what website that's probably going to be about you and you'll have little or no (mostly no) recourse about what kind of content they will be posting there. Do yourself the huge favor of avoiding a potential headache down the line and go and invest in buying your domain name today.

If you're birth name is somewhat formal, I highly recommend buying that name, too. For example, my birth name is Thomas (not Tom). Because I don't want anyone using www.thomasgurnee.com for any content that is related to me without my consent, I bought this domain name for myself as well. As it happens, I do not use www.thomasgurnee.com for any acting purposes, I use it for my photography, but I rest easy at night knowing that both of these domains are and will always be under my direct control.

Domain names are relatively inexpensive. Any ISP (Internet Service Provider) you choose to use (1and1.com, hostgator.com, godaddy.com, etc) will show you how much it is to register a domain with them. Typically, these prices are around the $5-10 range/year. However, most website packages that you must buy to host a website include a domain name within them so instead of paying for both a domain and package, you just pay the package cost. At this stage in your career, you may just want to go with the least expensive option and when your stardom (and bandwidth usage) increases, then you can upgrade for your needs. Or, sometimes the ISP companies have sales and you can get upgraded packages at a discounted price. Packages range in the $8 – 15 a month range but, for example, 1and1.com (my internet host provider) is having a sale where their mid-range package is available at $3.49/mo, pre-paid in advance for a year and you're allowed one domain name and you can build 3 websites with their website builder tool at 12 pages each. Objectively speaking, that's a pretty good bargain. I've been with 1and1.com for 4 years now and I like their customer service. But again, be sure to shop around and if you choose to go with an ISP that has a build-your-own-website option, be sure to find out what the monthly price will be for you to host your site with them.

When you sign up for a package, be sure to make your domain registration details <u>private</u>. This way, you protect your privacy and anyone who wants to try looking up any personal details via a "whois" or domain name search will only find your ISP company's details there. You don't want any stalker-type strange fans coming directly to your home's address do you? Some ISP's will charge you a $1 – $2/month extra service charge for this so be sure to read the fine print when you buy your domain name and list it as private.

When building your site, scout around other actors' websites and see what works and what doesn't work for you. You want your user to be able to navigate very easily to where you'd like them to go and not be confused while there. For certain, your home page needs to have your headshot photo(s) and contact details. After that, you should have any other images available, your resume, your contact details, representation details, your reel and an about you page. You can certainly add more pages if you'd like; it's your website! Make it as attractive and informational and as good of a marketing/representational tool as you can.

Finally, be sure to add Facebook, Twitter and YouTube links to your homepage. By networking in these social sites, the Internet spiders (as they are called) will see that your site has influence and will page rank you higher on the search engine sites like Google, Yahoo! and Bing. This basically means that anyone who, for example, goes to Google and searches your name will find your website popping up as one of the top ten links on the first search page. This is extremely important because you <u>always </u>want to pop up as high as possible on search engines. Why? Because page 1 placement is where 90% of Google click-through traffic comes from. Page 2 drives about 5% of clicks to a webpage and page 3, well, you don't want to be on page 3 because page 3 drives about 1% of clicks. So you see, if you're using a webpage to market yourself, you have to be on the first page of a Google search result.

Now, not only is it important for you to be on page one of a Google (or other search engine) result, you really want to be number 1, 2 or 3 on that first page because the top three links capture 61% of click-through rate traffic. That's freaking huge. Whether you're marketing yourself or perhaps a product or service (which, of course, your acting is – it's a product and service), it becomes tantamount to your business that your webpage is optimized to come up search result number one, two or three. There's a lot of information out there about "SEO (Search Engine Optimization"), and there are lots of people who can assist you with this, but be certain they're going to charge you a fee for their support. So, it's up to you. Build a site of your own and do some research about how to optimize it with the Internet spiders so you come up number one on a Google search, or pay someone out there to do it for you.

The Casting Couch: Ladies, I eluded to this before. If you take your clothes off for anyone with a video camera, there's probably a 99.9% chance you're video is going to find its way to the internet even if the videographer says, "Don't worry, it's just an audition." They'll say it won't go up on the internet, it's just for our files. Be very dubious about this comment. It's your body. You can do with it what you want. Just be ready and responsible enough to accept whatever positive or potential negative publicity that comes your way if you find yourself on an internet site in compromising positions. The casting couch is a real thing. If anyone in the industry asks you to take your clothes off to "give you a better shot at getting a role", they're probably a nobody and are just looking to influence you in any way they can to get into your pants. Please don't be naïve enough to go for this crap and never let anyone drive/take you somewhere you don't want to go. Listen to your intuition and trust that there will be other auditions from straight-shooting people that will not exploit or take advantage of you.

Newsletters: Email newsletters are utilized by many actors here to spread the word about themselves and to keep them in the minds of those who matter. They work just like postcards but are free. The trick is to get an email list together and work or do something continuously enough that it warrants your making note about it. Make your newsletter lighthearted, make fun of yourself and be exciting. People like reading things that excite them and make them laugh. People tend to ignore statements that are simply neutral or bland. If you can, include pictures and/or video (Youtube) links because people are visual creatures and pictures tend to keep your audience captivated and interested.

Depending on you and your volume of work, a newsletter can be sent out once a week, monthly or quarterly. It's your newsletter. Make it what you want it to be.

Social Gathering and Events: It's always good to be seen in public. Make it a choice of yours to get out every once and a while and meet new people. You never know who you're going to run into. This being said, when you do go out, keep in mind your image. If you should run into a certain director or casting agent you've always wanted to meet at a Starbucks, are you going to be presentable enough to say hello? Image plays a big role here in LA. So when you go out, always be ready to introduce yourself, or be introduced, to someone that may be a decision maker.

Branding: Speaking of going out and taking your image with you... A big Hollywood buzzword around town right now is "branding". According to writer, director and producer Stephen Mitchell:

"Branding, development, marketing and management of actors are considerations to be given to an actor's career if he or she is to have one. The same applies to the careers of writers and directors."

Everyone has a unique brand. As an actor, it's up to you to define, establish, and then proactively and productively promote it.

"What, per se, is a brand," you ask? Consider Ferrari, the car company. Does the name already have you thinking about red, sexy, fast and expensive automobiles? Have you already had thoughts about the prestige and perceived influence it brings to their owners? Anyone

104

who drives a Ferrari instantaneously has judgments made about him or her. The first of which is, they're rich because they can afford to drive such a car. That prestige, that air of speed, of sexiness, of success is Ferrari's brand at work in your mind.

Consider other famous brands. Coca-Cola, Wal-Mart, Kentucky Fried Chicken, Alka-Seltzer... Instantly, ideas pop into your minds about what these companies and products represent and stand for. Actors, too, have brands. When you think of Brad Pitt, do you think sex appeal? Do you think masculinity with a touch of danger? Even when he plays comical roles he still brings these traits with him doesn't he? Jack Nicholson... He brings a psycho edge to all of his characters, yes? And again, even to the comical characters he plays. Angelina Jolie. Sex appeal with a little tinge of grunge. These traits are their brands at work. Defining your brand is extremely important because it will quickly help establish what roles you're best at playing and immediately help others find out who you are as an actor.

For example: If you go into an audition and the casting person asks you, "So, tell me a little bit about yourself," how will you respond? This question <u>will</u> come up so will you better ready for it! Let me say that again: This question <u>will</u> come up. Is your answer going to be something like, "Well, I'm from Kentucky and I graduated with a bachelor's degree in Humanities there. I've done theater since high school and I can sing..." That's a nice answer, but reality is you're basically telling your auditioner that they can go on to the next actor because you're boring and not professional enough to be in that room yet. It was a decent enough answer, but what you simply don't know is that it's not what these people are looking to hear.

The nature of the question and the heart of what they really want to know is, "Who are you as an actor and why should I hire you?" Ponder this question because it's an important one. I'll repeat it: "Who are you as an actor and why should I hire you?" If you've never really given this type of question any thought, please do so now. You have to remember, it could be this person's job on the line if you end up being a total f*ck up. When someone asks you, "Why should I hire you?" they're basically asking in a nutshell, "Why should the producers put tens of thousands of dollars on the line in production costs, much less my job, if there's the slightest chance that you may fail miserably because you can't act, don't know what you're doing and have a terrible personality to work with?" That is what's happening my friends. Someone is putting tens of thousands of dollars in production costs betting that you are going to be great and give them what it is they're exactly looking for. Anything less, and you've wasted everone's time and money. That's why you absolutely must be on top of your game from the moment you step into an audition room to the moment that you wrap on set. They want the best from you and they're investing a lot of money that you're going to pay off for them.

So, let's revisit our previous question. You just walked into the audition room, you're on your mark, the camera goes live, you slate and the statement/question from the cameraman comes, "So, who are you? Tell me about yourself." You can either tell the cameraman and the person viewing your audition that you're from Kentucky, or, what would happen if you went into the audition and had a response like this, *"Well, I'm best at playing women who are intellectually and sexually predatory..."*

Whoa! Did you just have a reaction to that statement? Did it feel as if it came out of nowhere? It was certainly different, wasn't it? Don't you think you're going to get the immediate attention of this person sitting across from you with a statement like that? The first time I heard it, it had a shock affect on me and I immediately sat up and took notice. I said to myself, "Holy smokes, that's awesome!" This is your brand statement at work and you just let everyone in that room know who and what you are with it. Most importantly, you just distinguished yourself out from the other dozen (or hundred or so) other actors vying for the same role and you made them pay attention to you!

So who are you more intrigued with? The nice actor from Kentucky that can sing or the one that plays women that are intellectually and sexually predatory? How many times a day does the casting person hear average and typical responses like the one from Kentucky? Nothing against actors from Kentucky, of course. This is just a hypothetical scenario. How many times, on the other hand, will they hear a response like the one from the predator? Define your brand into a one-sentence statement and make it truthful about who and what you represent as an actor. When you do, you will immediately establish credibility in that room and if your acting is good, you will most certainly be remembered when that day is finished and have a better shot at getting a call-back.

Acting and career coaches here in LA know this and teach it to their clients. Their clients have good success rates at finding work compared to your regular Joe Blow actor out on the street because they've successfully focused in on who it is (the characters) they realistically portray. As I mentioned, Mr. Stephen Mitchell is someone I have been working with here in LA and I have learned an immense amount of information regarding the subject of branding and why it is so crucial to the establishment of my acting career. Stephen's career in the entertainment business spans over 40 years and I'm very grateful to be in his presence, listening and learning about how Hollywood works. Many of his ideas are ones I've incorporated into this book with his blessing.

Stephen is an absolute genius at deciphering who you are as an actor and creating branding statements for you. He created the sexual predator branding statement for a friend of mine and created mine as well. He offers private coaching (at very reasonable rates!) not only in branding, but in acting and helping to create your career outside of LA before you get here (remember the section about self-producing? Stephen can offer you lots of excellent information about this!). So, if you'd like to learn more, you can find him online here: http://emcpb.blogspot.com. Stephen is big into Ferraris so don't let the car fun he's written about on the site "steer" (haha, couldn't resist) you away from the acting information you're looking for there. Be sure to tell him I sent you!

Other career coaches I have learned from are Lisa Gold at "Act Outside the Box" – (http://www.actoutsidethebox.com) and Jodie Bentley's company, "Accelerated Artist" (http://www.acceleratedartist.com.)

Jodie's company is based out of LA and New York City and, among other things, they give workshops based on helping actors streamline-focus their careers. She and her coaches talk about the power of branding among other things. Oftentimes, they give free one-hour sessions as introductory courses but these free sessions always include useful and timely information. Remember, when you arrive or if you order anything from these nice people online, to make a note of it in your expense spreadsheet.

Something else to keep in mind when you go out is that your reputation goes with you. Are you a hard-charger party person that stays up until 3am and gets drunk at every party? Be honest, are you? That may be fine to some people, but for others it may mean you might not be trusted to be ready on set or ready to perform when you show up for your 6 o'clock morning call time. Some so-called new friends will want to introduce you to some fab party "extras".

Unfortunately, drugs play a role here in Hollywood just like everywhere else and it's up to you to decide whether you're going to choose to go down that path or not. It's your career; you can take it as seriously, or not as seriously, as you choose to. You can be on top of the world like Lindsay Lohan was a few years back, a starlet with great talent and great looks and a huge fan base, but when you start costing productions huge amounts of money because you're not showing up on time because your drunk or high or whatever, you're not going to be around for very much longer. I mean seriously, how many more movies and how much more money could she have banked if she had kept herself clean and not had to deal with all of her court nonsense? It's your career; it's your reputation. How do you want to be remembered?

Stage 32:

One final way I recommend to help market yourself is through the website Stage 32 (http://www.stage32.com). I was recently introduced to this site and I have found it very helpful in making new connections in the industry. The website is basically a Facebook for those of us in the entertainment industry and it already has over 125,000 members from all over the world. There's a lot of information being shared there and some fun anecdotes from our world. Sign up, it's free and start showing yourself off to everyone that's there.

All in all, the sky's the limit on how you can market yourself. These are just a few ways to help you get your career going. Be smart, be pro-active and be consistent. If you market yourself and keep these three important traits in mind while doing so, they will assist you in getting noticed. By utilizing the ideas above, you'll be sure to be ahead of the game. If you have other ways to market yourself that are successful and you'd like to share them, please write to me so that I may include your ideas (with credit to you) in the next edition.

Acting Bulletin Boards & How the Casting Process Works

Now that you have your photos and your resume and (hopefully) your reel together, it's time to start submitting yourself for auditions. For those actors out there that do not have agents, never fear, these bulletin boards will help begin to get you in the game.

There are a number of acting bulletin boards out there but the main ones to focus on are:

- Actors Access (www.actorsaccess.com)
- LA Casting (www.lacasting.com)
- Casting Frontier (www.castingfrontier.com)
- Now Casting (www.nowcasting.com)
- CAZT (www.cazt.com)
- Jeff Gund's Infolist (www.infolist.com)

Most of all the other bulletin boards out there in Internet land will be off-shoots from these and will be monthly-subscription based. As for now, in the beginning, you most definitely want to be subscribed as soon as possible to Actors Access and/or LA Casting.

Actors Access: Actors Access is one of the top two predominant actors bulletin board available. It's an offshoot from the original Breakdown Services and is still an integral part of the breakdown business. Breakdowns, for those that do not know, are the casting notices (the acting rolls that need filling) that film and television productions have. What happens is, in the morning, an agent receives the breakdowns (which is a list of all the current productions being made), that, in turn, list individually the number and type of actors needed for each production. When agents receive these breakdowns, they immediately go through them keeping in mind their lists of clients (their actors), to see who is right for which role. Next, they in turn submit their clients for possible auditions to the casting directors of those productions.

Back in the old Hollywood days, it was the agents themselves that had to go door-to-door and make their rounds to all the studios and read the scripts there that were written. They would make notes of the scripts they read (what rolls needed covering), come back to their offices and then go through their list of actors and submit those who were right to the studio casting directors. You can imagine what a long process this was. Today, obviously, it's all done by network computers. Breakdown Services was begun by a man named Gary Marsh and you can read a very nice little interview on how he began his business here:

http://www.iaemagazine.com/feed/vol1iss3/gary_marsh_breaks_down _services.html.

I highly recommend taking a couple minutes to familiarize yourself with this man and what he has done to change Hollywood.

Actors Access allows you to freely create a profile that includes the uploading of 2 photos and the posting of your resume. You may upload more photos to your profile for a $10 charge for each photo thereafter. After you've created your profile, you are free to peruse all of the casting notices that are posted online. If there is a notice that you think you are right for, you may click on that post and submit yourself to the casting director in hopes of scoring an audition for the role. For every role you choose to submit yourself for, Actors Access charges $2.00. If you submit your reel along with the photo you choose to send, your charge will be $5.00.

Obviously, the cost of submitting yourself over and over again will add up very quickly, especially if you're submitting your reels (which is a must as I'll explain in just a moment). So, Actors Access has a yearly fee of $68 you can purchase. After you pay this yearly fee, you are free to submit to as many casting notices as your heart desires (and include your reels each time) and there is no $2 or $5 fee for doing so. Therefore, every year you should make it a priority to dedicate $68 to Actors Access (make your spreadsheet notation!). Just think, after submitting yourself 34 times without a reel, everything you submit yourself for after that is free. Or, after submitting yourself just 13.6

times with your reel, you're submitting for free after that for the rest of the year. So, as you see, $68 for a year's worth of casting information in the grand scheme of things is not that much.

Now, why do you submit your reel with your photo? It's because the service gives priority to actors that do. That is, **all actors who submit themselves for a role and attach their reel for the casting agent to see, <u>get placed in line</u> *in front of* all the actors that submit themselves for that role that do not have a reel.** Do you now see why it is <u>so vitally important</u> to have a reel and have at least one that is uploaded to Actors Access? If it's still not clear, let me re-phrase.

When you submit yourself (your photo) to a casting director for a role, **if you do NOT include a video reel along with it, YOU GET <u>PLACED AT THE BACK OF THE LINE</u>** behind all the hundreds (if not thousands) of other actors who are also submitting themselves for that same role that <u>do</u> have reels. So, the most important lesson to be learned here is to get a reel up on Actors Access the same time you begin submitting yourself to casting notices.

As for reels, you must keep this in mind. As I've mentioned before, casting people do not have time to look at entire reels. So, the trick is to upload single 30 second (or less) clips that you have on video instead. Because a casting director can pretty much tell in about 10 seconds whether you can act or not, anything over 30 seconds is probably going to be overkill.

Breakdown Services charges $22 per every minute of video uploaded to them. Something that is not well-known to actors new to LA is you can take your entire reel (that is, your reel with all your attached scenes) to Breakdown Services and have them break it up for you into each individual clip. This way, you have the ability to individualize and tailor which clip the casting director sees.

Once you have your reels uploaded, you want to be sure to label them properly for casting people to see. Do not label your clip, "Demo Reel Clip". No. Instead, label it with meaning, like, "Strong, type "A" businessman who doesn't take no for an answer." Can you see how a casting person might take an interest in your clip versus someone else's generic, "demo reel" label? Can you see how your video would capture interest versus someone else's that has no description at all? Give them something to nibble and you might just get a bite.

How the Casting Process Works: Essentially, you have two batches of actors that submit for one single role. You have a group that submits with a reel, and you have a group that submits without one. The group that submits with a reel is put into a batch that is seen first by the casting director on the other end. The second group of actors without reels is still also available to the casting person to look at, but, if, and that's a very big if, the casting director needs to see the second group of actors without reels, you'll be lucky. This is because, chances are, there will already be a sufficient number of actors already to look through in the first group. Also, chances are, the casting director will not have the time to go through the second group of actors. Why not? It is because of the sheer number of submissions he/she receives.

While at a Breakdown Express meeting, our hosts showed us what casting directors actually see on their side of things. And what we saw was quite eye opening. From one example of a live post on their website at the time, it showed everyone in the room what we, as actors, are up against. What we witnessed was a casting call notice put out for a single television role. The posting was advertising the need for: "Male in his 30's, clean-cut, Caucasian, dad type, television under 5 role". In literally 3 hours, there were already 1,334 submissions. It's true. Of those 1,334, 1,168 were submitted with reels. In the first 3 hours! After 6 hours, the number was 2,713, 2,304 with reels. So, the question to you is: 1) do you think the casting director working this network show has the time to go through 2,713 submissions? And 2) do you think those who did not submit without reels would ever be seen? Personally, I feel sorry for those 409 actors that wasted their two dollars. Do they know they're wasting their two dollars? Probably not. Did this book just save you some money?

Continuing to use this example, here is what the Casting Directors see on their side of things. When casting directors post a job like the one above, you, as the actor submit for it. After a couple hours, or, whatever timeframe the casting directors give themselves to accomplish their task of finding an actor for their published post, they will begin looking at the number of submissions that have come in. What they see is your photo, sized 2x3, 5 images across and rows going infinitely deep down the pages. If the casting directors had 2,409 submissions of people (with reels attached) come in, they have 2,409 people to go through. Keeping in mind their time is very limited, how fast do you think they scroll through these photos? Yes, very quickly. That's one MAJOR reason your headshot has to stand out! If they like your look, they may select you and later on check out your reel. They may look at the notation that was written by you or your agent. If everything still looks good, they'll rate you on a scale of 1 – 3 and if you're in their top group, you'll get looked at again when they have finished (or have run out of time) going through the submissions.

Now, staying with our example, of those 2,409 with reels that submitted themselves (or had their agents submit them), for this example, only 536 were looked at by the casting director. That's right… Which means, the casting director did not have the time to go through all 2,409 – they only went through the first 536. Now, not only do you really have to feel for those souls that didn't submit without a reel, but, you have to feel for those actors who had a reel and didn't get a chance to be seen either. Did some of those actors not have yearly subscriptions and therefore paid $5.00 to be included into the casting call? Probably. Were they in the group of 536 that was looked at by the casting director? No one knows as I'll explain in the paragraph below. At any rate, are you getting a good feel for not just the importance of having a reel, but for the sheer scope of how many actors are out there? Boggles the mind, I know, but that's why I choose not to think about it and why I wrote that whole chapter on intention for you.

The good news is, for those that submitted "on time" – that is, the time between when the post first went live to the time that the casting director began making his or her selections, this group of actors are not seen in the order in which they submitted themselves. That is, if the post went live at 10:00am and I was the very first person to submit for that job, it would mean that I would be the first to be seen by the casting director, right? Unfortunately, no. In order to make it more fair for all those actors who submit "on time", Breakdown Services computers take charge and jumble all the actors that have submitted themselves and gives them to the casting director in no particular order (the only exception is they all come from the first group of actors that have reels). So, even though you were the first, or the last actor, to submit "on time" during the casting director's timeframe window, your chances of being seen are just the same as your fellow actor who also submitted on this role. Said in another way, it's basically up to Breakdown's computers as to where you randomly get spit out in the list of actors the casting director will see when they login. Of the 2,409 that submitted "on time", the first 536 actors the computer generated were the lucky ones the casting director had time enough to see and choose from.

If you happened to make it into the group of 536 and if your headshhot caught the eye of the casting director, when they select you, you'll soon be receiving a casting notice from Actors Access that you have "Cmail" pending in your account. Cmail is Actors Access's way of notifying you that you have an audition. Actors Access will proceed to email you a maximum of three times to notify you of this notice. If you're busy submitting yourself, be sure to check the email account you have set up with Actors Access daily so that you can be sure to receive any notices in a timely manner.

On another positive note, congratulate yourself on at least being selected! You beat out literally a thousand (if not more) other actors out there to get an audition. Celebrate this fact for a moment, congratulate yourself on having a headshot that gets noticed and then, get to work on your sides!

One final word about your audition. Since the casting director thought enough of you to come in for 10 minutes of their time to audition, show up for it! You'd really be surprised at the number of actors (that is, those who have been around a while) who get an audition for a small role they submitted for, who will then bail on going to the call! Seriously! Want to drive a casting director nuts? Submit for a role, get the audition and then not show up for it.

Think about it. Your slot in the audition could have gone to someone else. Perhaps that someone else was going to be perfect for the role.

Perhaps that person in that roll was going to get noticed by someone further down the line and picked up for even greater things later on. Because you were apathetic about going to the audition and you flaked on it, you just cost someone their slot at possibly not just getting the role, but starting a major career for themselves. Big deal, you say? Well, what if the casting director has another call that you're absolutely perfect for, that's a big role and pays well? What if this casting director has a good memory about past casting calls regarding those who don't show up for their auditions? As I've said before, it's really a small town here in Hollywood. You <u>will</u> see the same casting directors more than once. Do you think you stand a chance in heck at getting the role? Do you think that you'll even get so far as to get another chance at being called in?

Friends, it's called acting. **<u>Relish</u> every single opportunity** you have to act in this town. And that includes the opportunities you have to act at your auditions. Unless it's an absolute emergency and you can't make your audtion, bust your ass and do whatever it takes to get there on time (if not early) for it. Never, ever get complacent. Because as soon as you do, the universe will feel that you're not serious about why you're in this town and soon thereafterwards, you'll wonder why you're not getting anymore auditions. Always remember why you're here. Always remember how it feels to be here. Celebrate the fact that you've won a victory just by being selected to audition and show the casting director why they made the right choice by selecting you to come in and read.

<u>Virtual Channel Network</u>: The Virtual Channel Network (http://www.virtualchannelnetwork.com) is a subsidiary website of Breakdown Services and it offers free online video content for people in the industry. Almost all of the listed channels on the network are there to help actors in one way or another. For example, a channel called, "The Reel Deal" is hosted by a genuine working casting director and she and her guest host review demo reels that are uploaded. It's like a movie reviewing show, but with demo reels. It's quite fun to watch and very informative. Other channels have agents and managers talking about their line of work in relation to actors… There's a channel that gives tips about "the Business of Acting", etc.

It's worth it to check out this website and spend a little time on it once a week, or even once a day to help in your education process.

Casting About: One last subsidiary online company of Breakdown Services that is useful is called, "Casting About" (http://www.castingabout.com). Casting About is an online service that lists every current production that is in prep, casting or filming and lists every casting director and casting associate on that project. It incorporates a feature where you can select certain casting people to whom you would like to mail, and you can create and print out mailing labels for them. There are notes the researchers in the office make about each production and every production's address is certified by these people to be correct and up to date. Also, there's space provided for you to make your own personal notations.

Why is Casting About so important? Aside from the IMDBPRO.com, HCD and Director's Guild publications, this is another important online service that you can use to really begin to target and <u>focus on creating and establishing relationships</u> for certain casting people you want to meet and ultimately know. It's also an amazing tool to use whenever you go into an audition. For example, if you have an audition for a show, go to Casting About and look up all the casting people associated with it. Memorize these names and go into the audition knowing who everyone is. "Oh, you must be Sally James. I saw this is your first assignment as a casting "director". Congratulations."

When you go into an audition with this type of confidence, it shows and you're going to stand out. Set yourself apart from everyone else going in as just another actor by mentioning something unique to them (because you have "inside information") and they'll remember you. Follow up with a postcard or a thank you note and you've just begun creating a new casting director relationship. Continue to check in on this person in Casting About from time to time and when you see they begin a new project or climb the ladder from an Associate to a Director, shoot them a new note. I hope you can see how valuable this service can potentially be. Casting About services charge $9.95 a month (with automatic renewal! Be careful of this with your credit card!) or $48.95 for a year's subscription.

Be sure that if you choose to subscribe to any of these services now or in the future, that you record these expenses into your accounting spreadsheet!

LA Casting: LA Casting is the other top bulletin board service that is geared more towards commercials. Whereas Actors Access posts mostly theatrical listings, LA Casting is known to post a significantly larger number of television commercial auditions. In regards to overall numbers, LA Casting's listings are approximately 75% of what you'll find on Actors Access, but there are more paid opportunities. Whereas Actors Access lists many unpaid student projects and short films, LA Casting's listings are mostly all paid projects.

LA Casting charges $14.95 for month-to-month subscriptions. For a 6-month pre-pay, the rate is $59.70 and for a year pre-pay, the rate is $119.40. These rates allow you to submit yourself without limits to commercial, theatrical and print projects. If you do the math, you'll see they do not offer a discounted 6-month or yearly pre-pay rate so it's up to you on how much you want to pay now or later. NOTE: Single submissions are charged at $1.49 each and you're **still** charged this fee every time you submit whether or not you have a month-to-month or a year subscription. Said another way, even though you have a paid subscription with LA Casting, you still pay an additional $1.49 for every time you submit yourself for a posting.

LA Casting works the same way that Actors Access does. You do NOT know how many actors are also submitting on the same role as you. You do NOT know how many of these actors the casting directors will look at and you do NOT know whether you will be seen or selected. So just because you pay $1.49 to submit yourself for an audition, do NOT expect to be to be seen by the casting director, much less be called in to read.

On a side note, once you successfully find yourself a commercial agent, they will be the ones submitting you to commercial casting posts. Hence, no more need to pay the yearly or individual submission fees.

Casting Frontier: Casting Frontier is a lesser acting bulletin board. There are postings here but only about 10 - 20% in numbers compared to Actors Access. They offer a free profile with one photo and resume upload and free submissions. Premium services include their "Premium Profile" ($6/month or $36/year) that allows for 5 headshots to be uploaded to their servers and a link to your website. Another "Premium Profile Plus" ($10/month or $60/year) package, allows for 10 headshot photos, 1 actor reel and a link to your website.

As you submit to roles using this service, when you are called into an audition, bring a Casting Frontier "barcode" with you. This barcode allows them to instantly access your online profile and saves them time during the check-in process. Once your profile is finished and you've uploaded all of your information, it's a good idea to print this barcode ID for yourself and have it with you at all times. I recommend either putting a copy of this barcode into the batch of resumes you keep with you in your car at all times (hint, hint) or laminating the barcode and keeping it in your wallet or purse.

CAZT: CAZT (http://www.cazt.com) is another small bulletin board whose quantity of postings are about the same as Casting Frontier. Many of their projects are deferred pay or no pay, but on occasion a good feature or commercial or paid pilot rolls into the mix. Many of CAZT's postings may be found on other bulletin boards and so you'll find that although you may not be a member of CAZT, you'll still end up going to their studio to audition.

CAZT sets itself apart from the other bulletin board services by having/allowing the casting directors give feedback on your auditions. CAZT uploads your audition video to their website so you can later view how you did, though they do this for a price. They do allow you to read the comments of the casting director for free, but only in return for a Facebook posting that their website does on your behalf (it basically states that you had an audition at their studios).

What you end up paying for is the ability to submit on listings and the access to view your audition. Their Premium Membership allows you to watch your audition videos online and allows you to send these auditions to your agent, manager or coach. The service runs

$14.99/month plus a one-time $5.00 setup fee. Or, they offer a 3-month pre-paid package at 28% off for $35.97, or finally a 6-month pre-paid package at 44% off for $53.94.

CAZT is located adjacent to a DMV (Department of Motor Vehicles) facility and the two building structures appear the same. CAZT is located at the end of this structure towards the back. For first timers, it can be confusing to find. The best place to park is on Formosa street, or a block or two away. Be sure to allocate a little extra time to find parking due to the DMV being busy. Beware of the street signs there, too. Formosa Street and some of the parking areas only allow you one hour parking. Also, Formosa turns into a one-way only street near the entrance to the structure so don't go the wrong way or turn into the street going in the wrong direction.

Typically, most of the auditions I have attended there I have been in and out of in one hour or less. However, there have been times I've been there over one hour so be very diligent about setting an alarm on your phone to keep your car from getting a ticket. The best thing to do is when you arrive at your audition, set your alarm and then see how long the line is. If it's long, go re-park your car to one of the two-hour streets nearby. Reason being, you won't have the worry in the back of your mind that you're risking getting a parking ticket by not being out on time. You need to be absoultely focused on your audition and only on your audition. Hence, and this goes for any audition you go to, give yourself the gift of peace of mind. Do yourself the hugest favor by 1) getting to the audition early, and 2) finding a good, safe parking spot that allows you more than enough time to go in to your audition and come out of it stress free regarding the time you've had your car there. You'll be very glad you do this each and every time you go out.

There are other bulletin boards besides these four, but these others are basically knock-off copies and they'll charge you monthly fees to access them. Be wary of these boards, especially if you find them advertised on Craigslist. The difference between these knock-off boards and Actors Access and LA Casting is the timeliness of the information. The information on the knock-off boards will be the same, but the time frames for submitting yourself will be old. That is, you may be paying a cheaper monthly rate, but most of the jobs on these boards will already be a day old and sometimes this is all it takes for the job to already be closed. Hence, even though you may be submitting yourself on this cheaper bulletin board for a role that was also on the bigger four sites, it won't matter because the casting director has already made his/her selections and closed the post.

That's why when submitting on the four major boards, you do so in a very timely manner. The sooner (meaning the same day a posting goes out) the better. Anything after that and you risk leaving yourself out in the cold, so to speak. Also, as for the knock-offs, be sure to inquire about them before signing up and get lots of references from fellow actors to find out if they're legitimate or not. Finally, remember, if you pay a monthly fee to access any bulletin board, they will charge your credit card automatically every month. Don't get caught short if you're near your limit or are out of funds and should you ever leave LA or actin, be sure to cancel the subscription!

One last note about Breakdown Services. You may come across people from time to time that offer to sell you "the breakdowns". What they're "selling" is the list of breakdowns that are delivered to all the agents and managers every morning. Those that sell this information usually charge people $30/month for it. The problem is, it's not legal to sell these breakdowns to anyone that is not a licensed talent agent or manager and it's a practice that Gary Marsh goes after fervently to prosecute. The "dailies" as they're called, are nice to receive but, as I just mentioned to you in the last paragraph, you never get them on the day they're put out, you'll only get them the day after.

Hence, if you called or wrote to your agent inquiring about a role you'd be perfect for on xyz project, they're going to know you're getting the dailies because you'll be calling them about old news and calling about something that they've already (hopefully) submitted you for. If you write or call your agent about old news from the dailies you're receiving, you'll only be interrupting their job of finding more rolls to submit you for. So don't waste your money and don't waste your agent's time. It's nice to see what's being produced out there but is it worth opening yourself up to a lawsuit when you can get the same information via Casting About at 1/12th the price?

Jeff Gund's Infolist: (http://www.infolist.com) A gentleman by the name of Jeff Gund back in 2000 began his bulletin board list by helping out a few friends in acting by letting them know of casting opportunities he was hearing about. Before long, he incorporated all of the news he was accumulating into an "information list" and sending it out to his friends. By the time he decided to put all of his information online, he had a list of 7000 people to whom he was actively sending information to. I believe that list now tops some 20,000 people or more.

Jeff's Infolist is a great way to stay informed about a huge variety of things that includes casting info, workshops, events happening in and around town, jobs, music industry information and more. I highly recommend you register for his site (it's free!) and begin receiving his emails. You'll get a really good feel for everything that's going on around town and maybe once and a while, you'll find yourself responding to something you've received.

IMDB and IMDBPRO

For those of you who are not aware, the website IMDB.com (along with the more professional version IMDBPRO.com) is the number one website to find information on anyone in our industry. It's basically the Wikipedia for the entertainment business. They have daily stories on what's news in the industry; they list box office tallies, rankings and a whole lot more. Need to find an actor, or what he/she was/is in, or information on a movie or project? You can probably find it here.

IMDB (www.imdb.com) is the free site. Use this to find all your general information. You can create a user profile there but honestly speaking, it won't do you much good. You won't be able to upload a photo or list any of your credits. In fact, I recommend not creating a profile for yourself until you are ready to invest the money to buy the IMDBPRO yearly subscription.

IMDBPRO (www.imdbpro.com) is the twin, paid-subscription service website ($19.95/month with free 2-week trial. One-year subscriptions are offered at a 37% discount for $149.99). The difference is, on IMDBPRO, you are now allowed access to their industry directory, you can browse their In Production lists and see your "Starmeter" rankings. (Starmeter rankings are the website's way of providing a snapshot of who's popular based on the searches of their users). With the PRO version, instead of having a blank photo picture listed under your name that the free IMDB version "allows", you can now upload a reel, headshot and resume.

Before I get back into what "rankings" is all about (which a lot of actors think is a very important facet in their career), the main reason and way to use this site is for research. For example: every time you see a television show, at the beginning, you see actors' names appear. These actors are commonly the guest-stars that are appearing on the show for that week. Experiment some time and take note of some of these actors when you watch your favorite shows and look them up on IMDBPRO. Once you do, you can find out, for example, who their agent is, or, if they have a manager and you'll see their credit list. Ask yourself, have they worked a lot before getting this role? If not, then perhaps their agent is one who hires clients without many credits.

Also, that may mean the casting director of the show is one who also in turn, doesn't mind hiring actors that don't have many credits. Make note of their name. Look up their details. Perhaps this may be a person you might want to begin a networking/mailing relationship with... Looking to mail out to agents or talent managers? Look them up and see how many clients they have. Have their top 5 talents worked a lot this past year? If not, do you think they're working hard for their actors? Maybe, maybe not. Do they have clients that look like you? If not, they may be in the market for your look. If they do, maybe they send a lot of actors with your look out on auditions... At any rate, this is how to properly and intelligently use this site to your advantage and how to make it pay off for you.

As for rankings, though most casting agencies won't take these into account, once you begin to become popular, some will then begin to do so, especially if you're being considered to play a role for a feature film. It's been said, too, that some managers and talent agents take rankings into account before they choose to take someone on as a client.

The best way to ensure your rankings are in the four to five digit mark, is to have a lot of credits under your belt and make sure they are listed as credits for you on the IMDBPRO website. The more credits, the higher your ranking. For new actors out there, this whole ranking thing can be an emotional rollercoaster if you let it get to you. One week you're in the 5-digit range (10,000 – 99,999) and the next, you're pushing 7 digits in popularity. Since these rankings are updated every week, if you don't have a lot of credits to post or don't have traffic visiting your credit pages (or your home IMDB page itself), your rankings are going to take wild swings in direction.

Going from a ranking of 100,000 down to 3 million in one week is a perfect example of this crazy system they have. The pitfalls of having such a low ranking number is once a ridiculously low number is registered in their system, there's no way to take it out and it shows up on their ranking maps for the rest of your career. This is why I do not recommend immediately creating a profile for yourself under the IMDB site until you're ready to pay for the PRO site. From the very first day you create your profile, the site's algorithms begin to track your popularity and the rankings begin. If you're not popular and people are not clicking on your name or profile, be prepared to have beginning ranking in the millions.

What do you do about this? Well, if you're just starting out, my advice is, don't sweat it. It's not something to get all wrapped up in. But, that being said, there are ways to manipulate the system. Remember what I wrote about SEO (Search Engine Optimization)? The same applies to this website. Recently, IMDB incorporated a Facebook link into their grand scheme of things. When you go to an actor's homepage on IMDB, on the lower right side of their page, you can now Facebook "like" that actor.

When you do "like" an actor on your Facebook page, an IMDB notification will appear. In return, IMDB's internal website mechanisms see that someone has visited your page and this, in turn increases your popularity ranking. Also, when someone visits your individual credit pages, your rankings go up. Obviously, you can't ask all your friends to constantly visit your credit pages or "like" you over and over again, so some enterprising souls decided to do something about this and created a website called, "Karmalicity". http://www.karmalicity.com.

What the Karmalicity folks have done is set up a way for actors to help market each other on the IMDB ranking structure. Using a point system, you earn points by visiting and "liking" actors' IMDB pages and conversely, you give points away by having someone come and "like" your page(s). You can "like" people's IMDB credit pages, you can "like" their Facebook pages, you can follow people on Twitter and subscribe to people on YouTube. Every one of these actions earns you points and, conversely, you share your points with others that visit and follow or subscribe to you. In a nutshell, it's an ingenious way to ensure that there's a steady stream of people visiting your IMDB page(s) so that your rankings won't take drastic mood swings and they'll remain relatively stable and high. The best part is it's free to use, or there is a premium subscription service.

When you sign up, they give you a free week of "Premium" services, which means you're allowed 60 "actions" per day (i.e., going to someone's IMDB page and liking them would be 1 action. Visiting another actor's IMDB page would be 2 actions, etc.). After this initial week's time, you can pay a monthly ($6), three month ($15), six month ($24) or yearly $45 fee to keep these premier services, or, you can revert to the lowest grade of services that are still free. The difference being the free services allow you to receive 20 daily actions instead of 60. However, for every referral you bring to their website, they give you a free week of Premium services and you accrue points for doing so. So give it a try. It's a great way to learn about IMDB and about other actors out there. You might even make some new friends if you try networking (reaching out to others) on the site. If you think this information is valuable to you, please type in my referral link to the website into your browser bar and hit return:

http://www.karmalicity.com/b/?r=4372

Or, of course, you can browse directly to the site on your own and just leave off everything after the .com. Thanks!

Stay Current on the Trades – Or, Read, Read, Read

Part of your due diligence as an actor should be to read, read, read. As much as possible. Stay current on the trends of the business, keep up on who and what's hot, how the industry works, what's getting green-lit, etc. Obviously, there are the television shows that cater to this sort of thing, as Entertainment Tonight and Extra do, but a lot of what they broadcast is gossip and "baby bump", inconsequential so-called news. The "real" news that I'm referring to is the stuff about the movers and shakers of the industry.

Why should you bother? Well, obviously you don't have to, but in general, who are the people you're more likely to have fun conversing with? Someone who knows what he/she is talking about, or someone who's totally clueless? Well, maybe the latter is more fun for you but in this town being informed and having something intelligent and timely to input into a conversation gets you noticed. And since this is the industry you've chosen to devote your life to, shouldn't you take some time to get to know it?

Most of the trades have websites that provide news there for you for free or you can buy their subscription print magazines. Many other websites have come along that provide timely and worthwhile news on the industry as well. Here's a list of some trades and websites that you should follow:

- The Hollywood Reporter (www.hollywoodreporter.com)
- Variety (www.variety.com)
- IMDB (www.imdb.com) & (www.imdbpro.com)
- Entertainment Weekly (www.ew.com)
- E! Online (www.eonline.com)
- BackStage West (www.backstage.com) - focus on the "West"
- TheWrap.com (www.thewrap.com)
- IndieWire.com (www.indiewire.com)
- Deadline.com (www.deadline.com)
- DailyActor.com (www.dailyactor.com)
- WGA.org (Writers Guild of America – www.wga.org)
- DGA.org (Director's Guild of America – www.dga.org)

Other items of note to read are casting director and agent blogs and entertainment job bulletin boards. Casting Director Mark Sikes writes a weekly entry for Actors Access called "The Casting Corner". Bonnie Gillespie, another Casting Director, writes a featured column called, "The Actor's Voice". The point is, there are a lot of good people in the industry that are genuinely there to help and the insight and information they're sharing can be valuable in helping you make decisions and keeping you informed. Be open to these materials when they come to you, bookmark them and refer to them when you have the time.

If you're looking more towards other entertainment career avenues, two industry job bulletin boards I like to follow are www.entertainmentcareers.net and www.projectcasting.com. These sites have numerous entertainment oriented job listings, are easy to navigate and do include castings. Google search "entertainment job (or "career") Los Angeles" and all of the major studio links to their job boards will pop up for you. Be sure to go through at least the first 3 pages of Google links regarding the different sites that come up, instead of just the first page!

Auditions!

So now you've got an audition! Celebrate for a little bit - and then get to work! There are many different types of auditions so being prepared (as much as you can) will not only help give you a leg up on your competition, but also help calm your nerves when you go into the room. Being prepared means downloading your sides - if there are sides for the audition ("Sides", otherwise known as "copy", refers to what you'll be reading during your audition. It's the words of your character that are on the written page that you verbally speak and act out.) Showfax.com is a major source that will be providing sides for you. Once you have your sides, it's up to you on how you prepare your scene.

Most of the auditions you'll be attending will go something like this. You walk into a crowded office space and sign in. Sometimes you wait, sometimes you don't. Once your name is called, you'll walk into a room with a gent or a gal that welcomes you. They tell you where your mark is (the place where you stand) and then they will go and stand behind a video camera. When they say, "slate", you slate (to "slate" is to say hello and state your name. I.e., "Hello. My name is ____.") and then when they say "action!", you go. That's pretty much it. It's just you, the camera and the person running the camera.

Other times, the casting director is actually there and they have an assistant or two helping them. The casting director will sit behind a desk and watch you perform while their assistant films you. Pretty simple.

The point is rarely, these days, will you have a first audition where you won't be performing for a video camera. What should you take from this information? The knowledge that a video camera is a "thing". That is, instill in yourself the knowledge that a camera is not alive and that it is not going to hurt you. Hence, there's no need to be nervous or afraid of it. It's a thing. Period. Keep your power and go in and do what you do.

As for the audition process, always bring a headshot with resume attached (if not two) and your Casting Frontier barcode. Sometimes the auditioners will take a copy of your headshot from you, sometimes they won't. But always have it just in case. I did mention that you should always have at least two in your car at all times, didn't I?

When you do audition, **always** hold your copy. It makes the casting director (if they're in the room) nervous if you do not. Seriously. I've met many different casting directors and they <u>all</u> say the same thing. During your audition(s) – primary and call-backs, hold your copy. Why? Because if you flub, you won't waste their time by asking for a line or asking where you messed up. If you have your copy in hand (even if you have everything super memorized), it puts them at ease and they can now focus on your acting, rather than being afraid you're going to mess up and then ask them what line you're on. You want these people totally focused on you and your acting, right? Hold your copy.

Next, when you are finished with your audition, politely say, "Thank you," and leave the room. Do not ask to go again, do not ask, "Was that good?" and do not stand there. Say thank you and leave. If they want you to do it again another way, they will immediately let you know. If they do not say anything, leave, and let them call you back if they want to see more. Most of the time you'll get a, "Thank you very much," and that's it. Never expect any type of critiques on your audition; they don't have time to give it. Do not ask for another go. They don't have time for it. Simply leave and get on with your daily business.

Basically, this is good audition etiquette and it serves you well and serves them well to follow it. You don't waste any of your time and you don't waste any of theirs. The reason being is if you do waste their time, they're going to remember it and they won't think kindly of you the next time you come into their space. I've said it before, it really is a small town and you will see these casting directors more than once in your career, if not within the same year.

During an audition, <u>never</u> apologize. It shows weakness and sub-consciously tells the person auditioning you that you're ill prepared. Instead, if you flub, politely say, "**Excuse me, let's run that again.**" Take 2 – 5 seconds (no more! The camera is still running!), get recomposed and immediately go again. This is the <u>only</u> time you ask for a re-do. Memorize that line. Because you will flub in an audition and the natural thing to say when you mess up is, "I'm sorry."

So. End of audition and you've left the room. Did you do well? Great. Move on. Did you blow it? Great. Move on. The point is, the less you dwell in your head about how you did, the better off you are mentally. There's absolutely no reason to beat yourself up over a bad audition. If there's something you can learn from it, something you can maybe do better next time, then either make a mental note or even better, jot your thought down in a journal you keep regarding your auditions and don't do it next time. But move on. You'll save yourself a lot of personal grief by not moaning and groaning to yourself (or worse, to others) about your bad audition. Simply said, life's too short to cry over spilled milk.

Keeping an audition journal is a good idea. Besides writing down the information of the person you auditioned with, making notes of what happened may give you a heads up down the line for what you're doing right and what you're doing wrong. For example, maybe you have a tendency to talk softly. Were you loud enough? Were you projecting enough energy into the scene? Were your hands glued to your sides or your feet glued to the floor? You are actually allowed to walk and move around providing you have the space to do it and you've asked the camera operator what the limit of range of motion is. So did you use the space or stand there like a statue? After a few auditions, if the same issues keep coming up, by keeping a journal of your experiences, you'll be able to see and correct these problem areas. Work to resolve these things in acting class. Conversely, what did you do right? What did you do that proved to knock their socks off? Write those things down, too, and after a few auditions, take note of what has been working for you and continue to reinforce those good habits in future auditions.

Another good reason for keeping an audition journal is to notate who the casting director was. Though you may not see them in the initial audition room, by writing their name down, you'll be able to see after a while who's beginning to call you in on a regular basis. See someone who's called you in a few times? Start writing to them using postcards. Send a thank you note for the audition. Include them in a newsletter email. In other words, if they seem like they're beginning to establish a relationship with you, perhaps it's time to begin establishing a relationship with them on your side of things.

By keeping record of the casting directors that have been calling you in, you also may have good ammunition for a potential agent you may get signed with. At the beginning of the year, sometimes agents ask their actors to provide them with lists of casting directors, directors and producers you have worked with in the past so that they (your agent) may begin honing a working relationship with that person on your behalf. If you have such a list, you're much more likely to have your agent working hard for you versus not being able to do as much for one of their actor clients who does not. Remember the story about Jen Lilly and the book of casting directors she had auditioned for? This again, is a perfect example of why keeping an audition log for yourself is a good idea.

Finally, regarding the directors who later watch your auditions, you'll never really know what they want or are looking for. You can go into an audition and just blow it away. I mean really nail it. You leave flying high just knowing you'll get a call back. But it never comes. Conversely, you'll think what you just did was one of the worst auditions you've ever had and there's no way in the world they'll call…and then the phone rings. The point is, just make your choices, do what you do, forget about it and leave it up to the Gods after that. Don't worry. If there's something there they like, you'll probably be getting a callback.

Callbacks are nice things when you get them. It means you've gone from a pool of over a thousand actors, down to a few dozen, down to maybe a handful now. Celebrate again! And then get back to work. Callbacks can be intimidating – but only if you allow them to be! What typically occurs now is, instead of it just being you and the camera guy or gal, it's you, the camera guy, the director, his/her assistants, the producer, maybe someone from the company itself if you're doing a commercial, the casting director and his/her assistants… I've walked into a room where there were 10 people in it; all sitting behind desks and every single person had a laptop computer in front of them. I've heard stories of there being two tables on each side of the room that each had 6 people sitting behind them and the actor had a tiny 10x10 foot space to work in-between them. All you do, is mostly just what you did before. You go in, say hello, slate and then knock their socks off again. When your audition is over, say, "Thank you very much," and... That's right, leave. Same deal. If they want to work with you some more, have them initiate it. If not, you did your best. Move on and if the stars were aligned for you, you'll get a phone call. There's no reason to treat a callback any differently than your original audition. If you do, you're probably putting too much pressure on yourself to perform and it will show. Just go in, do your thing, say thank you, and leave.

One last thing regarding call backs, wear the same clothes you did when you auditioned the first time. This helps the casting people and/or director remember you and remember how your first audition went. If you wear something different, the auditioner may subsconciously strain to remember who you are and what you did your first go round. In the director's mind this puts you a step behind another actor who they will be able to readily recall that looks the same as they remember them being.

"Tell me about yourself": Every once and a while the people behind the camera may ask you a question or two. And the most dreaded of all questions, "Tell me about yourself," usually pops up. As I alluded to before when talking about branding, you need to be prepared for this. Once again, they are not asking where you are from, how many siblings you have or if you love acting. What they typically want to find out is what do you represent as an actor.

What you'll also find during auditions is that sometimes after the ones you totally nail, the auditioner will want to chat with you to find out more about you. Aside from blowing his mind away with your branding statement, you should be prepared to chat a little by having something else lined up to say that's smart, brief and tells them about your personality. For example, what do you do for fun besides acting? Know thyself and be ready with such an answer.

So really, what do you do for fun outside of acting? Actor Jen Lilly has it down pat. When she's asked this question, she immediately responds she likes to flip furniture. She says she buys crap furniture on Craigslist, refurbishes or restores it and then sells it again at 10 times the price. She also mentions she loves to eat and bake. That's it. She's kept her response brief and to the point, she's responded in a likeable and friendly manner and she provided them a door to enter through to ask her more questions about her if they want to. So know the things that you like and what will be comfortable for you to answer.

This is the chance to have some conversation on a human level and it gives you an opportunity to get present and be relaxed. Do not respond, "Well, what would you like to know?" That's the standard-issue, "I don't know what the hell I'm doing," answer and nothing makes you look more boring than not being able to say what you're into. Be prepared to create the relationship!

How do you become friends with someone you've just met? You ask questions of them. They're simply doing the same thing, it just so happens there's a camera in the room with you. Give them something they can cheer about from you! Give them something that sets you apart from the rest. Be ready for this question and be confident and forthwith in your response when it comes. They want to like you and they want to like working with you. No one wants to work with a dolt or someone they don't like and this little conversation can and/or may be the defining point on whether or not you get the job. Give them the opportunity to see the likeable you and to say yes!

"What roles do you fit?": This is another question you should really take some time to consider. Not only for answering during an audition, but for answering in an interview with an agent or manager. Agents have a tendency to ask this question because they really want to know if they have a place for you within their company. They also want to know if you're a serious player that has actually put some thought into this question.

Remember the workshop I spoke of that had us trading our piece of paper with the 25 different character types on it? This is where that

134

exercise comes into play. "What roles do you fit," is a very important question for your career. It helps you really hone in on who you are as a person and who you can seriously portray as an actor. Do some homework here. Find some people who can be straight up with you and ask them, without prejudice, how they really see you.

This might be a little awkward at first and your ego may have conniptions about this, but you have to seriously understand that, what you think you can play, and how others see you, may be totally different. What comes out of this, however, is gold. And that gold is, when you have an absolute and realistic vision of who you are, there's inner peace and a rich, quiet confidence that you begin to subconsciously radiate that becomes irresistible to others. In acting, there's really something about simply "being yourself". Letting your inner beauty shine through and into your character is what makes a great actor great.

Find out who you can really play and get specific about these areas. Don't simply stop at, "The mid-western housewife". Go deeper into who you are and expand on this woman. "The mid-western housewife whose life is lived for her children but who inside is secretly torn by her conflicted desires to see the world. I get charged up about these kind of roles…" Now you're on to something. Now you really begin to "feel" the richness of who this person is. You're stating and drawing a picture of your brand. Delve deep, spend the time, ask the hard questions and come out with the rich answers. And when you're asked, "What roles do you fit," you can knock them for a loop with how confident you are in yourself and your being.

Auditions are weird things. Every one is unique. Heck, every person you meet is unique, right? Some people will like you, some won't. About all that can really be said is just go into an audition, do your best and let the chips fall where they may. Move on after you've left the room and get busy working on getting and nailing the next one.

Finally, send a thank you card or postcard to the casting director that called you in. Get in the habit of doing this as soon as possible when you get home so you don't put it off and then it's too late. Research who they are and write down their business address before you leave for your audition. Some actors keep postcards in their car that are pre-stamped and when they finish their audition, they quickly jot down a quick note, "Hi ____, just wanted to say thanks again for having me in to play (role) in the (production name) audition. I appreciate it!" and then they drop it in the nearest mailbox. Whatever you write, make it brief, say thanks, and sign your name. Work that relationship because others out there won't and the next time you may be right for a role with this casting director, you may be the one they remember and call in again.

Building Your Wardrobe:
I've harped on how much this town is going to wear on your pocket book because I'm really trying to prepare you for what kind of financial reality you're going to be facing here. From the rents, to the gas pump, to class fees, etc., as I've said before, there's always someone or something that's out there that wants to grab your money. One glimmer of hope though that won't take too much of a hit on your wallet is, interestingly enough, suplimenting your wardrobe.

Most everyone loves to shop for new clothes. I'm no exception. However, the idea of paying $45 for a new pair of Wrangler or Levi jeans from a large retailer like Target or Walmart leaves me quite irked. I always thought paying $20 for a new long-sleeve shirt from JCPenny or even Ross was a good deal until I found the crown jewel of resale stores here in LA: "It's a Wrap". (http://www.itsawraphollywood.com)

This one recommendation will help pay for this book over and over again.

"It's a Wrap" is a resale shop that gets all of its clothing from actual TV and movie sets and they claim they are the only store on the planet that does this. Not that that last little tidbit is important or anything, but what is important is that you're going to be buying articles of clothing for auditions that best suit the character brands you play most. For example, one of the character brands I play best are lawyers/politicians. Therefore, I go to "It's a Wrap" and find new, high-quality long-sleeve shirts and ties there that go well with my suits. No matter what character you play best, "It's a Wrap" will have clothes there that range from pants, shirts, shoes, ties, dresses, blouses, coats, belts, hats, gloves, hankies, costume jewelry, etc, etc, to suit you and all of these items come literally direct from the shows and movies that are shot here in Los Angeles. Pretty cool, huh? But what's really exciting is the prices they have for most of their inventory is way, way, I mean <u>way</u> marked down! And, the clothes they bring in and stock are practically new! In many cases, they are brand new - they've literally never been worn and sometimes these articles still have the original tags on them from where they were purchased.

For example, what this means is, a wardrobe assistant on a tv set or movie was given an assignment of going out and buying some shirts or pants for one of the actors on the show he/she was working on. This person went out to different shops (many being quite decent – ie, Abercrombie and Fitch, Gap, American Apparell, etc, etc), bought up some different shirts/pants/coats/suits/jewelry, etc., and brought them back to the set. Something from the lot of clothes may have been selected for the actor and that actor may have worn those articles for a scene. Since most of the time the actors are not allowed to keep the clothing they wear on set, those articles are then sold off at ridiculous discounts to "It's a Wrap", who, then in turn resells these items to people like you and me.

Since there are so many tv shows happening here in town at all the various studios and all the clothing you see your favorite actors in has to remain fresh, up to date and new, the articles that show up on the racks in the store are just that – fresh, up to date and (practically) new!

What's even more exciting (!) is some of the fashions that come in are made from honest to goodness real clothing designers. For example, I found a V-neck short sleeve t-shirt made by John Varvatos. Ohhh, it was a brilliant deep blue color, the material was something you just don't find in the retail world and it just oozed richness. I had to have it. The price tag however, was a bit rich (this happens with the designer stuff at the store), $35. Thirty-five dollars for a nice shirt may not seem all that expensive to some people, but when you're skimping by just making ends meet, a price like this for a simple t-shirt of all things can make one pause. What got me over the hump though, was the sale the store was having that day. Fifty percent off!

And they do this type of thing all the time. When you sign up to be on their mailing list, they will notify you of the special sales they have a few days in advance and many of those sales are 50% off. Sometimes the sales are for one item at 50% and then everything else 30% off. Or sometimes, the entire men's line or women's line is 50% off. Sometimes, the whole store is 50% off! What's even better still (!) is some things that don't move are marked down even more – down to 75% off. How about that? And I'm telling you the 75% marked down stuff is still top of the line.

When I got home, I was quite curious about this "designer" t-shirt I bought, so I looked it up online on Mr. Varvatos' website. Would you believe that t-shirt I bought retailed for $195! A t-shirt (!), for $195?! Ha ha, yup. And I picked it up, practically brand new for $17.50. Nice, huh?

Just last week I went in and picked up two pairs of pants, one a nice pair of tan Abercrombie and Fitch and the other a slim pair of jeans. Both new as far as I could tell, both 50% off with the sale the store was having meant I scored them for $10 each. Sweet.

Folks, for your auditions, and many times for the roles you'll be playing, the casting directors will want you dressed in solid colors with no visible labels. You can find a lot of these type of things at "It's a Wrap" and these items won't come anywhere near breaking your bank.

"It's a Wrap" has two locations. One up in the Valley in Burbank and the other on the westside just outside of Beverly Hills at Robertson and Pico.

If "It's a Wrap" isn't enough, another jewel in the pile is the National Council of Jewish Women thrift stores (http://ncjwla.org/council-thrift-shops/). There are a few around town, but the best one always seems to be the one on Santa Monica Boulevard. This is probably because it's the closest one to Beverly Hills. While the clothing selection doesn't quite have the amount available to you that "It's a Wrap" has, it can still be quite worth stopping in. You really just never know what you're going to find in this place clothing wise but honestly speaking, every time I've been in the store I've always been able to find something pretty swanky for literally pennies on the dollar. My best score to date was two Armani long-sleeve shirts, both in excellent condition, $6.00 each. Yup. Armani for $6.00. And oh, do they fit so nice.

For you ladies, a gal pal of mine scored a real leather sachel bag (I mean, this leather was n-i-c-e!) None of that fake stuff. Ten bucks. She loves boots and shoes. Same thing. What appeared to be new items, real leather, barely if at all worn, $15.

Lastly, Goodwill resale stores are a plenty here in Los Angeles. One can find a lot of decent clothing at Goodwill but what strikes me most of the time are the articles are much more worn looking than what you find at "It's a Wrap" or the Jewish Women's thrift stores. Goodwill is Goodwill. People donate their used items there. And Goodwill being who they are, most of the items are fairly well used.

When and if you shop at Goodwill, keep in mind the location of the store. For example, if you're shopping at a Goodwill in the Valley, chances are the items there are going to be sub-par. On the other hand, if you're shopping at the Goodwill in Santa Monica, the items there are going to be more upscale and probably better quality. What I find too, are the prices at Goodwill can sometimes be a bit up there for a resale shop (most mens shirts I find run in the $8 - $20 range). I, personally, have found that I'm able to stretch my dollar much further frequenting the other shops I've mentioned and I usually get a better return (in quality of garment) for my money. All in all, it's up to you on how frugal you choose to be and of course, how far you choose to travel to do your shopping.

So there you have it. If you're prosperous enough to do your shopping on Rodeo Drive and happy to spend $4,200 for a pair of jeans (I've seen it – no joke!), then by all means please do so and have fun doing it. For the rest of us that haven't made that transition to the upper echelons of life yet, be kind to your wallet and try shopping at the resellers a time or two before you visit that clothing chain or mall retailer again. You just might be happy you did.

Booking a Job!

Your phone rings and there's this weird phone number on it (or, maybe your caller ID says your agent is calling you!). You know you've been to a couple of auditions recently so you answer it and then there's a voice on the other end that you don't recognize asking for you. I don't know about you, but these are the kind of phone calls I like! The person on the other end introduces him/herself and you hear the lovely sound of the word, "producer" when he/she gives their title to you. Congratulations, when calls like that come, it usually means you've booked a job!

There are a couple things to remember about phone calls. First off, always have a pen and paper next to or near your phone. Next, you're in the driver seat. They like you and they want you. Be courteous and start asking questions. The first one you'll probably ask is to have the person on the other end remind you of the project they're working on. Face it; you've been to a handful of auditions that week. How would you know what project they're calling you about? Simply ask them to remind you. You'll remember once they tell you.

After they remind you of what project it is you just booked, some time during the call it's important for you to inquire about the rate. You want to confirm the pay you'll receive. Also, inquire as to the release they're going to want you to sign. Though this is something they may have made notations about in the audition posting, you need to be clear what "in perpetuity" and what a "buy out" means if that's what they're asking for.

In Perpetuity, means once they have your signature on the contract and have you on videotape, they can then run that tape until the end of time if they choose to and they are not obliged to pay you one thin dime more than what you agreed to in that original contract. Know those infomercials that you see on Saturday mornings or afternoons over and over again? Do you think those actors are making residuals for every time they show up on the television? Think again. Most of those actors are probably non-union and were paid $100 for their time and signed a "buy out, in perpetuity" contract. Beginning actorswill do almost anything for work and companies out there know this. For you ladies out there, are they asking you to do a nude scene? If so and the contract says, "In Perpetuity", is your roll going to be worth having your naked body potentially show up again and again and again in all different forms of media? Is what they're paying you up front going to be worth it over the long run? It will happen.

A **"Buy Out"** means that you have agreed that one lump Sum of money to be paid for your services is all that they are required to pay you. After that, for however long they choose to run your spot, especially if it's 'in perpetuity', they may do so and you will not be entitled to any more pay in any sort of way.

Here's a perfect example. Do you remember the infomercial regarding the little blender called "The Magic Bullet®" from a couple of years ago? Well, they have a new, upgraded version called the "NutriBullet®". I was booked to be a part of this non-union, buy-out infomercial. When they began marketing the stuffing out of that product, my face was being shown all over the United States in many different markets over and over and over again.

While watching TV, I saw myself on 3 different television channels, at 3 different times on 3 different Saturday mornings. My friends all over the country have seen me on other channels at all different times of the day. Am I receiving a residual paycheck for every time this infomercial runs - like a union actor in a union production would? Nope. All I can do is sit back and smile and be grateful this infomercial goes on my resume.

Furthermore, I found out from my mother (who ordered the product), that there is a hardcover recipe book that is included in the order. Inside of that book are pictures of the actors that were portrayed in the infomercial. And yes, yours truly is included. You can find me drinking a wonderful organic fruit and vegetable concoction on page 132 of the first printing. Were any of us paid for our images they used in the publication? No we were not. These are the pitfalls of being non-union and signing "buy out" and "in perpetuity" contracts.

Unfortunately, it's a tricky spot. You want to work, gain those credits, make some money... But for a measly $100 that TV show or commercial spot is going to use you and run your roll again and again and again and there's nothing, unfortunately, you can do about it. It happens. Non-union productions typically know that talent comes last on the totem pole and they pay accordingly.

All in all, it's a decision you have to make for yourself on whether you want to put yourself out there for what amounts to $10 - $15/hour. Hopefully, you'll score bigger projects later on, but for the meantime, be prepared for what comes along when you see or hear those words, In Perpetuity and Buy Out.

After confirming your rate and buy-out details, and if you have agreed to do the shoot, be sure to write down the name of the person who called you and their contact information. Also, if different from the person you are speaking to on the phone, write down the name and title of the person you will need to find on-set. Get your shoot location and call-time details and immediately mark your calendar. If your character did not have lines during your audition(s), always (!) ask if there are sides you'll be needing. Obviously, if there are lines (or were during your auditions) you will need to have these lines ultra-memorized and a part of your character. Finally, confirm if you need to bring any of your own personal items for wardrobe considerations. After that, say thank you, hang up and celebrate!!

Be Kind

The old adage of being kind to strangers really applies here in Los Angeles. Hollywood is a small town and though there's so much going on, the industry itself is small and those working in it all have the memories of elephants.

When you move to Los Angeles from out of state, especially from the Midwest, there's a huge culture shock that you have to be prepared for. Like New York, where I've lived, Los Angeles, too, is a tough town to make a living in. People who grow up here grow up with tough exteriors. For those that are blessed to not only grow up here, but to have grown up in privileged families, many do not know the struggles of moving to LA and finding work to "make it".

People, unfortunately, do not wave hello from their cars when they pass you; they don't wave hello on the streets. Just a few days ago I was speaking with a friend at a small conference and a woman came down the stairs a few feet away. Knowing she needed to come through where we were standing, I politely moved out of the way. Not once did she make eye contact with me, nor did she acknowledge in any way that I did her a small favor. Was it rude of her not to say, "thank you," or register my movement in any way? That's up for you to decide. My point is, there's an attitude of entitlement that comes with the territory when you live here and you have to be aware of when it comes up. There's a fine line between being bold and being arrogant. You'll find a lot of the latter here in Los Angeles.

What you must remember though, is to be kind. To everyone you meet. There are dozens of stories that author Napoleon Hill, in his great book, "Think and Grow Rich", conveys about the power of kindness. I recommend you buy this book and read it a couple dozen times. Really. Because what it comes down to is this: you just don't know who you're going to meet in this town and that person may hold the golden key to your career in their back pocket. By being nice and helpful, you increase your chances of a magic door opening for yourself.

Being kind, however, does not mean sacrificing your principals or letting people walk all over you. You are a human being that is endowed with the same unalienable God-given rights to life, liberty and the pursuit of happiness just the same as everyone else. Just because they may have been a little (or a lot) luckier than most in becoming financially and/or professionally successful in their lives sooner, does not give them, or anyone, the right to treat you in any way that would be demeaning or would make you to feel inferior.

By acknowledging your true self and having self-confidence, you alleviate the possibility of being in this sort of situation and you will appear more attractive. Being kind makes you even more attractive. Standing your ground and being firm in retort (all said in a respectful way), goes a much longer way at earning respect with decision makers than by becoming a quiet and simple "yes" person. Conversely, no one really likes to deal, much less work with, a belligerent hothead.

Be kind to others and be kind to yourself. Stand your ground. That's the way to get noticed on a positive level in this town. Bring that "certain something", that charisma, that everyone likes to be around and those magic doors will begin to open for you.

Support

Along with our everyday needs, you must remember something very important. Take care of yourself. And take care of your Self.

Los Angeles is a great city. But it's one that can suck the soul right out of you if you let it. People can be wonderful and people can be real jerks. Times can be tough when you move to a new town and when you don't have anyone to fall back on. Loneliness becomes an unwelcome and uninvited guest. Your choice to move here is a large one and it's a mighty leap forward in your life that I truly commend you for.

During that leap, I believe it's important to find that something extra that you can fall back on that gives you that little bit of extra hope to keep the fire burning bright within you. I've been here a few years now and there have been times when the world seemed like it was going to cave right in on top of my head. People were being rude, bills were coming due, my car was acting up… And all of this was happening at the same time. I got so down even my dog didn't even want to be around me (well no, that's not true). It's times like these when you question your own decisions. I'm here to tell you, there's a place to go to rejuvenate your spirit and where you can find the uplifting need of fellowship and love. That place is in Culver City (close to LAX) and it is called Agape.

Reverend Dr. Michael Bernard Beckwith founded the Agape Spiritual Center 25 years ago and for those of you who have seen the movie, "The Secret", Reverend Michael is the African-American gentleman with the dreadlocks who was featured. Agape and Reverend Michael have changed my life for the better and for the first time in my life, I truly believe I found a real "home" to go to on Sundays.

Just as the body needs good food to sustain itself, I believe the soul, too, needs a good place to go so you can remember what true living is all about and enable your inner being to expand and evolve. Agape is a non-denominational center that focuses on the growth of the soul and it is a house of unconditional love and gratitude. It is the perfect place, I think, to go to give your Self a mighty lift. You can visit

Agape at the following link and if you're still out there contemplating your move from wherever you are, you can watch the Reverend and services online via the link, too.

http://www.agapelive.com

Obviously, there are other places of worship here in Los Angeles and I suggest you to seek them out. Agape, for me, is a place where I can feel truly connected to everything again. When I do feel connected, I feel like I'm unstoppable. Find a place of your own where you can re-energize your inner being and you'll be much more apt to weather the challenges that come around every once and a while. Plus, while you're there feeling good again, you never know who you might meet. Just sayin'.

© 2009 LISA ANN WILSON

In Conclusion

As we part, I want to thank you for buying my book and I sincerely hope that you have found it useful. I hope the information I have provided helps with your decision making process. If you do choose to make the move, I wish you the best of luck with your acting career and I hope your transition is a smooth one. You'll find the acting world here quite enticing and exciting!

Below, I leave you with a blog link written by actor, Jenna Fischer (otherwise known as "Pam Beesley" on the television show, The Office). Jenna's story is the consummate one of how an actor's life can be here in Hollywood. Her's is one of struggle, but with persistence, it all pays off in the end. Just as you've so kindly done with my book, please take the time to read her advice online. It will help bring great clarity to what I've written and what you potentially have ahead of you and your life by pursing an acting career.

In closing, just remember to <u>have a plan</u> before you come and even before you arrive, put it into action! <u>Be conscious</u> of your decisions and actions. Set goals with a timeline. Make sure your choices and decisions come from your own mind and not someone else's. By staying congruent with your plan, you can assure yourself that you're moving in a straight line to success, rather than taking the long and winding road to it.

If you have any comments you would like to make and/or success stories along the way, I would love to hear them. Until then, I wish you the best of luck and I look forward to seeing you on the set!

Best of Days!

Tom Gurnee

comments@movingtolaforacting.com

"The Acting Advice Blog" – by: Actress Jenna Fischer.
(Copy the link into your browser or simply Google the title above.)

http://www.myspace.com/pambeesley/blog/141657788

CPSIA information can be obtained
at www.ICGtesting.com
Printed in the USA
BVOW06s0127200117
474025BV00006B/88/P